HISTORY-SOCIAL SCIENCE FOR CALIFORNIA

OUR CALIFORNIA

WILLIAM E. WHITE, Ph.D.
PROGRAM AUTHOR

PEARSON
Scott Foresman

EDITORIAL OFFICES
Glenview, Illinois
Parsippany, New Jersey
New York, New York

SALES OFFICES
Needham, Massachusetts
Duluth, Georgia
Glenview, Illinois
Coppell, Texas
Sacramento, California
Mesa, Arizona

ISBN: 0-328-16672-3

35 16

Contents

CALIFORNIA REPUBLIC

A Book About California

California state seal

Did you know that California is home to the largest tree in the world? The General Sherman Tree grows in Sequoia National Park in our state. California is home to many plants and animals, as well as people from many backgrounds. California is also your home. Maybe you have lived here all your life. Maybe you have just moved here. Either way, there are probably many things that you still want to learn about our state.

This book—*your* book—is about California. Like our state, it is special in many ways.

General Sherman Tree

First, you can write in it. As you read, you will fill in time lines and find places on maps. Sometimes you will answer questions by circling or underlining the text. Other times you will write your answers in the text.

Second, every unit in your book begins with a Study Journal. On these pages you will write what you already know about California, as well as what you learn about our state.

Finally, you will find many photographs and drawings of the people and types of land that make up California. You will see how California has changed over time.

What You Will Learn

Your book begins by explaining how Earth is mapped out and how to find places on maps. This knowledge will help you understand the maps throughout the book. You will also learn about the geography of California, including its land, water, and weather.

Once you are familiar with our state's land, you will learn about its history. Our story of California begins hundreds of years ago with the California Indians. Then people from Europe and the eastern United States started to come to this area. Their ways of life were different from those of the California Indians. How did these groups get along?

Next, you will explore the reasons why different groups of people came to California. Many opportunities attracted people here at different times. Some people came after gold was discovered. Others arrived during and after the building of the railroads. Still others were interested in the movie industry.

As our state changed, so did the kinds of people who moved here. As a result, the people of California have come from a variety of backgrounds. Together, they have shaped our state's history and will continue to shape its future.

This map shows the different areas of California that share similar features.

The church of San Luis Rey de Francia shows the influence of the Spanish in our state.

Many Japanese came to California in the 1800s.

It is a big job to keep California running smoothly. In the last unit, you will learn about the laws that guide our state. You will also study the people who make these laws, those who see that the laws are followed, and the people who decide if the laws have been broken. Some of these people work for communities in California. Some work for our state. Others work in Washington, D.C. All of these leaders help the people of California.

The Next Step

Are you ready to learn more about California's natural features and valuable resources? Are you excited to uncover the history of California's people and how our state has grown and changed over time? As you read, you will begin to see how these changes and developments have affected your life. You will also learn how you can help our state continue to grow and move forward. Turn the page to begin our journey into the story of *Our California*.

These dancers are celebrating the Mexican holiday of Cinco de Mayo at a Los Angeles festival.

Name:

Study Journal

In this unit you will learn how Earth is divided and how to locate places on a map or globe. You will also learn about the many different parts of our state and its cities. Complete the activities on these pages as you read the unit.

What I know about . . .

the part of California I live in:

What are the regions of California?

On the map below, outline the four regions of California you are learning about.

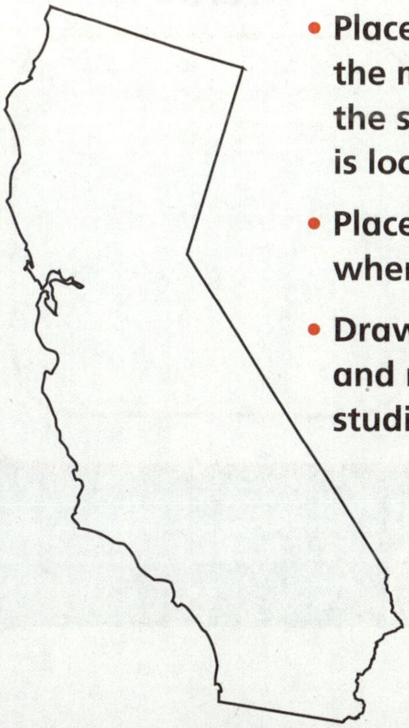

- Place a star on the map where the state capital is located.
- Place a black dot where you live.
- Draw landforms and rivers you studied.

On the lines below, describe two California regions other than the one where you live.

1. Region:

2. Region:

Complete these sections as you read the unit.

On the globe below, draw and label the following:

- equator
- prime meridian
- Tropic of Cancer
- North Pole
- South Pole
- Tropic of Capricorn

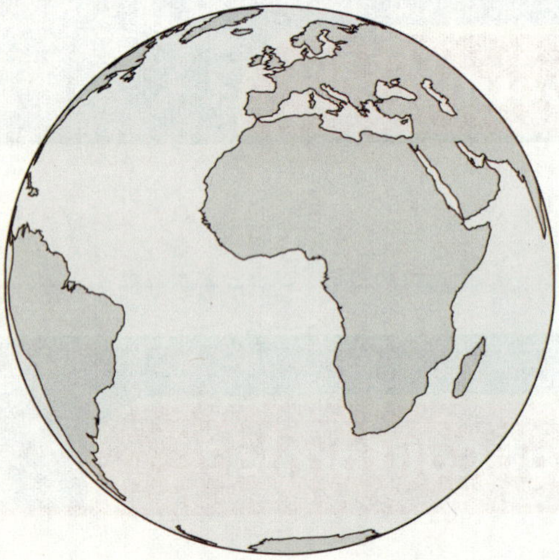

Circle two items below and explain how you might use them to describe your location.

- longitude
- absolute location
- latitude
- hemisphere

Item 1:

Item 2:

Draw a picture of each of these three types of communities.

urban | **suburban** | **rural**

I have learned . . .

Name:

H-SS 4.1.1 Explain and use the coordinate grid system of latitude and longitude to determine the absolute locations of places in California and on Earth.

How do you locate places on Earth?

CONNECT TO YOU How do you tell someone how to find a place? You could give the person the name of the place, such as *Ridgecrest, California.* Or you could give its location. Ridgecrest's location is about 36 degrees north, 118 degrees west. What do you think these numbers and directions mean?

Preview the Lesson

Vocabulary

compass rose *(n.)* a symbol that shows the main directions on a map

line of latitude *(n.)* an imaginary line that runs east-west around Earth

line of longitude *(n.)* an imaginary line that runs from the North Pole to the South Pole

absolute location *(n.)* the exact or nearly exact location of a place on Earth using degrees north or south and east or west

equator *(n.)* the line of latitude that circles the middle of Earth

prime meridian *(n.)* Earth's main line of longitude

Vocabulary Activity Circle the vocabulary word above that describes the feature you would use on a map to find direction.

Reading: Main Idea and Details

Reading Skill

A *main idea* tells what the paragraph is mostly about. Writers often include a topic sentence that explains the main idea. Other sentences give supporting details that tell more about the main idea. As you read the lesson, underline the topic sentence in each paragraph.

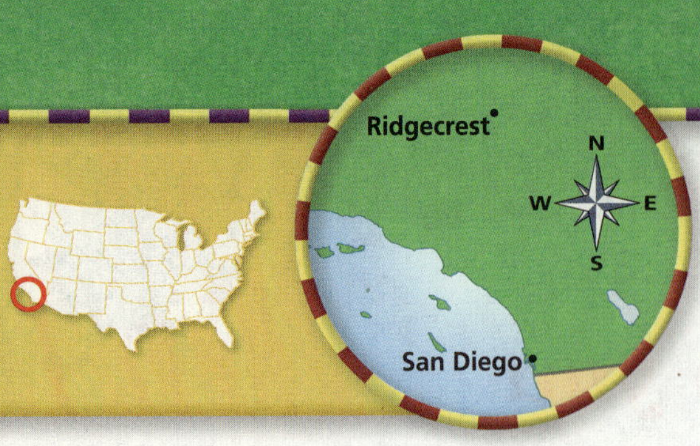

Directions

Directions are important in locating a place on a map. If you look at the map of part of California above, you can see that Ridgecrest is north of San Diego. North, south, east, and west are the main, or cardinal, directions. Cardinal directions are often shown on a map using a compass rose. A **compass rose** is a symbol that shows the main directions on a map.

Latitude and Longitude

Another way to locate a place is by using latitude and longitude. A **line of latitude** is an imaginary line that runs east-west around Earth. A **line of longitude** is an imaginary line that runs from the North Pole to the South Pole. These lines form a coordinate grid system, or a series of crisscrossing lines, on globes or maps. Both latitude and longitude are measured in degrees (°).

1. Main Idea and Details **What are the cardinal directions?**

2. Main Idea and Details **In what direction do lines of latitude run?**

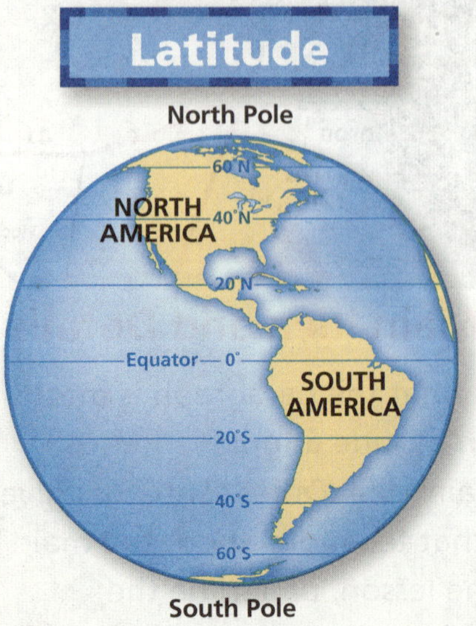

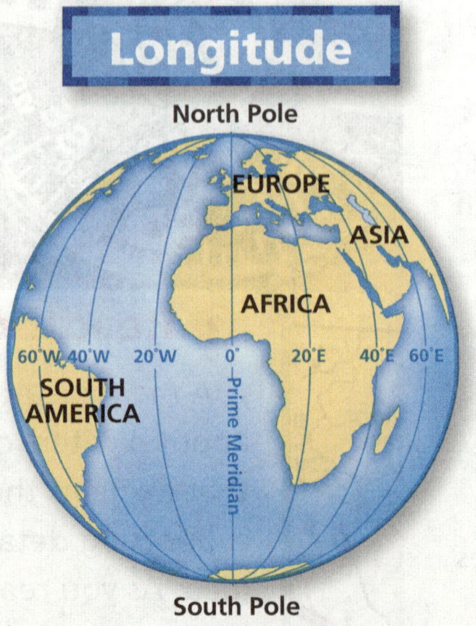

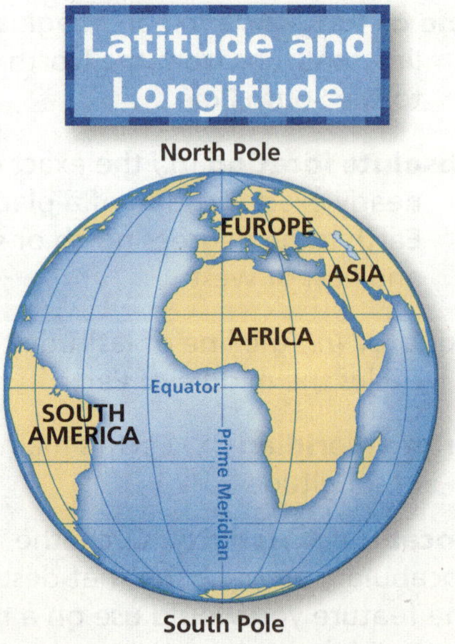

On the third globe, trace a line of longitude.

Trace the line of latitude and the line of longitude that comes closest to Ridgecrest.

Absolute Location

Every place on Earth has an absolute location. **Absolute location** is the exact or nearly exact location of a place on Earth using degrees north or south and east or west. The absolute location of a place is made up in part by its degree of latitude north or south of the equator. The **equator** is the line of latitude that circles the middle of Earth. It is the starting point for measuring degrees of latitude. Since Ridgecrest is about 36 degrees north of the equator, part of Ridgecrest's nearly absolute location is 36°N.

The absolute location of a place also includes its degree of longitude east or west of the prime meridian. The **prime meridian** is Earth's main line of longitude. It is the starting point for measuring degrees of longitude. Since Ridgecrest is about 118 degrees west of the prime meridian, the other part of Ridgecrest's nearly absolute location is 118°W. The absolute location of Ridgecrest is written as 36°N, 118°W.

3. Why would it be helpful to know the absolute location of a place? *Evaluate*

Summary

Maps and globes have tools to help us find locations. Describe how latitude and longitude help you find the locations of places on Earth.

Skill

Latitude and Longitude

Learn More On a map that shows latitude and longitude, it is easy to find a place's location. For example, Los Angeles is located at about 34°N, 118°W. To locate it, find the line of latitude 34°N on the right side of the map below. Then find the line of longitude 118°W along the top of the map. Trace each line with your fingers until they meet. That point is very close to the absolute location for Los Angeles. Very often a place is not located exactly where a line of latitude and longitude meet. You may need to find the nearest lines to such a place in order to find its location.

Try It

Use the map to answer the following questions.

1. **What city is located near 39°N, 123°W?** *Identify*

____

2. **The entire state of California falls between what two lines of latitude?** *Analyze*

____

3. **What are the closest lines of latitude and longitude to Fresno?** *Apply*

____

Name:

H-SS 4.1.2 Distinguish between the North and South Poles; the equator and the prime meridian; the tropics; and the hemispheres, using coordinates to plot locations.

Lesson 2

How is Earth divided?

CONNECT TO YOU You have learned how to plot lines of latitude and longitude to find the absolute location of places on a map. You can also use some of these same lines to divide Earth into sections. Suppose Earth was an orange. If you cut the orange at its equator, you would have top and bottom halves. You could also cut the orange through its poles. How can these sections be used to describe locations on Earth?

Preview the Lesson

Vocabulary

hemisphere *(n.)* one half of Earth

climate *(n.)* the weather patterns in one place over a long period of time

Tropic of Cancer *(n.)* the northernmost point where the sun shines directly overhead

Tropic of Capricorn *(n.)* the southernmost point where the sun shines directly overhead

Vocabulary Activity Circle the words above that describe specific locations on Earth. Underline the words in each definition that tell how they are different.

Reading: Main Idea and Details

Reading Skill

Writers include *details,* or more information, to support the main idea of a paragraph. As you read page 8, number the details the writer included in the first paragraph about the North and South Poles.

The North and South Poles

The North and South Poles are located at opposite ends of Earth. The North Pole is a point in the northernmost part of our planet, where all of Earth's lines of longitude, or meridians, meet. The South Pole is at the southernmost point, where these lines of longitude also meet.

Through the center of Earth, connecting the North and South Poles, there is an imaginary line called Earth's axis. Our planet spins around its axis once every twenty-four hours. This motion is what creates night and day.

Dividing Earth

Our planet can be divided into very large areas called hemispheres. A **hemisphere** is one half of Earth. One way to divide Earth in half is along the equator. The area north of the equator is called the Northern Hemisphere. California and other states in the United States are in the Northern Hemisphere. The area south of the equator is called the Southern Hemisphere. Most of South America is in the Southern Hemisphere.

Earth can also be divided from the North Pole to the South Pole, along the lines of longitude known as the prime meridian and the 180th meridian. The half that goes west of the prime meridian to the 180th meridian is called the Western Hemisphere. The United States is located in this hemisphere. The Eastern Hemisphere lies east of the prime meridian to the 180th meridian.

1. Main Idea and Details
What is the main idea of the first paragraph?

2. The state of California is located in what two hemispheres?
Draw Conclusions

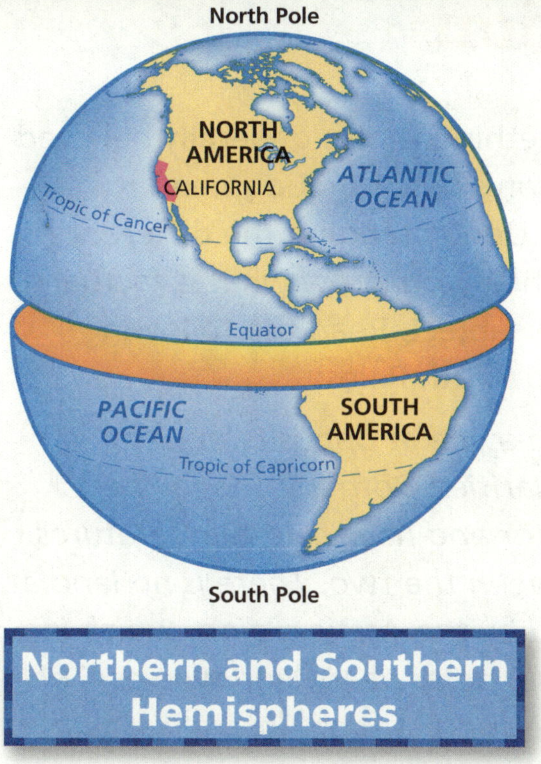

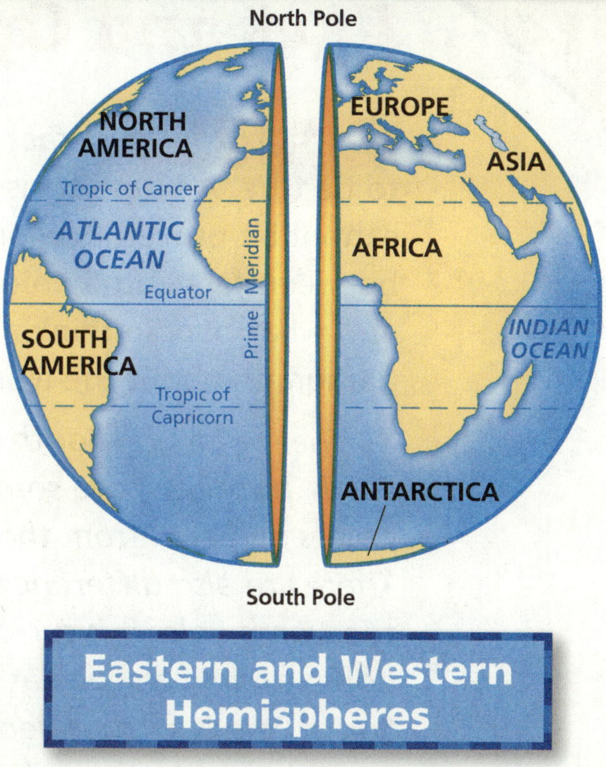

On the left-hand globe, mark the Northern Hemisphere with an *N* and the Southern Hemisphere with an *S*. On the right-hand globe, mark the Eastern Hemisphere with an *E* and the Western Hemisphere with a *W*.

The Tropics

The climate in different areas of the world depends mostly on how the sun's rays shine on Earth at different latitudes. **Climate** is the weather patterns in one place over a long period of time. Places at or near the equator always have a warm climate because sunlight shines almost directly down on those areas all year long. Places near the North and South Poles generally have colder climates because the sun's rays hit those areas at an angle. From that angle, the rays bring very little warmth.

The areas near the equator that receive the most direct sunlight are called the tropics. The **Tropic of Cancer,** at about 23°N, is the northernmost point where the sun shines directly overhead. The **Tropic of Capricorn,** at about 23°S, is the southernmost point where the sun shines directly overhead.

3. Main Idea and Details **What are the tropics?**

Summary

Places on Earth can be located in many ways. We can locate places in relation to the poles or within hemispheres. Describe the location of your community using the terms *hemisphere* and *pole*.

Skill

Fact and Opinion

Learn More A *fact* is something that is generally believed to be true. An *opinion* is a person's belief or judgment. It cannot be proven true or false. Understanding the difference between fact and opinion can help you know what is factual and what people think about a subject. Read the following paragraph about the North and South Poles:

The North and South Poles may be at opposite ends of Earth, but they have some similarities. Both are the farthest points on Earth from the equator and have cold temperatures. There are also differences between the two. There is no land at the North Pole. It is surrounded by the Arctic region, which is home to animals such as caribou, polar bears, and whales. The South Pole is surrounded by the continent of Antarctica. Seals and whales live there. It is also home to many kinds of penguins, which do not live in the area around the North Pole. Penguins are the most interesting animals. Therefore, it is better to study the South Pole than the North Pole.

Try It

Look at the list of statements about the North and South Poles below. Decide which statements are facts and which are opinions. Then mark an X in the correct column.

	Fact	Opinion
Whales live near both poles.		
The North and South Poles are at opposite ends of Earth.		
Penguins are the most interesting animals.		
It is better to study the South Pole than the North Pole.		
The South Pole is surrounded by Antarctica.		

Name:

Lesson 3

H-SS 4.1.3 Identify the state capital and describe the various regions of California, including how their characteristics and physical environments (e.g., water, landforms, vegetation, climate) affect human activity.

How are the areas of California different?

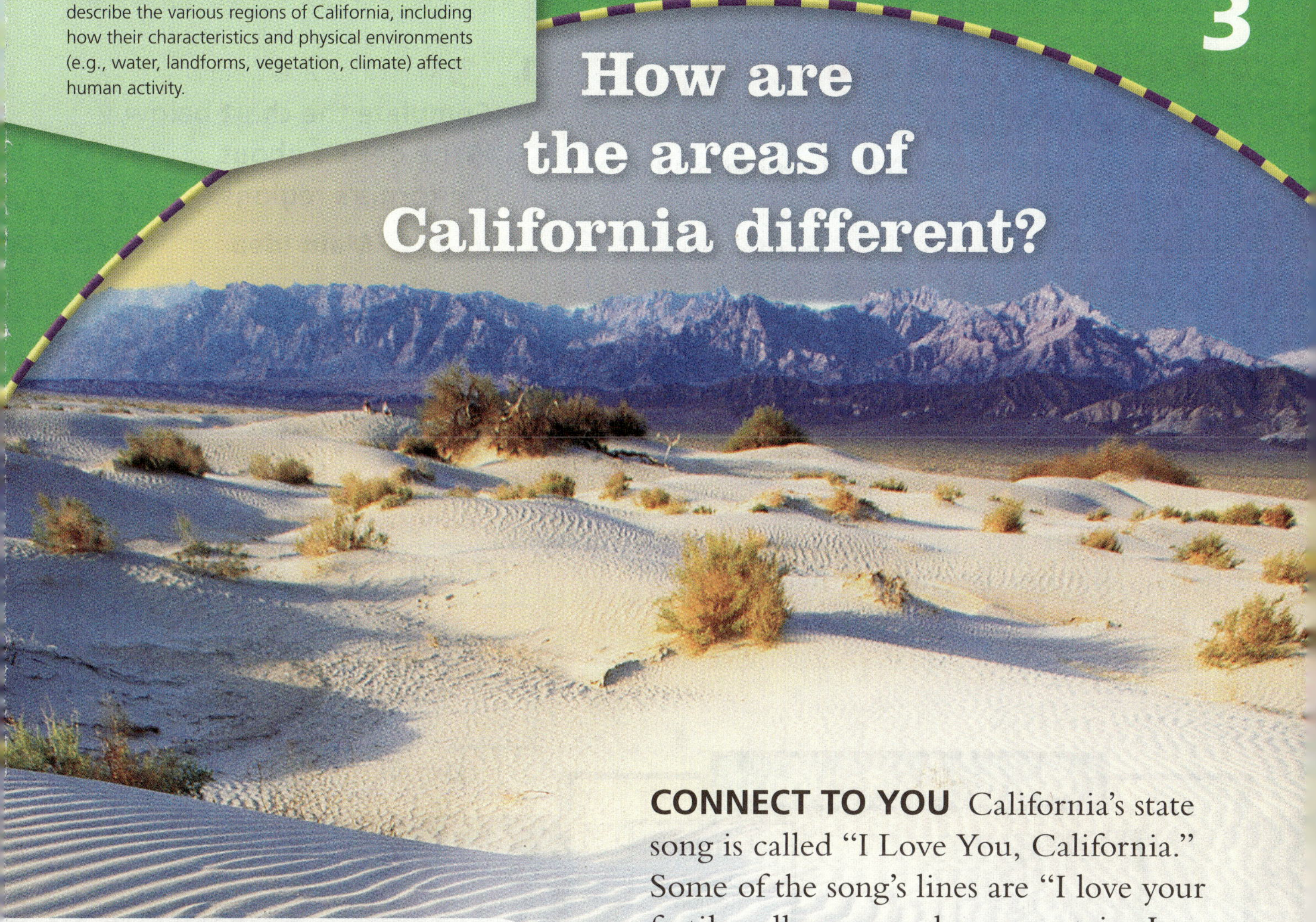

CONNECT TO YOU California's state song is called "I Love You, California." Some of the song's lines are "I love your fertile valleys; your dear mountains I adore . . . I love your grand old ocean and I love her rugged shore. I love your redwood forests—love your fields of yellow grain . . . ." What do you love about California's beautiful land?

Preview the Lesson

Vocabulary

region *(n.)* a large area in which places share similar features

landform *(n.)* a natural feature of Earth's surface

capital *(n.)* a city where a country's or state's central government is located

coast *(n.)* the land along an ocean

desert *(n.)* an area that receives less than ten inches of rain in one year

Vocabulary Activity Underline the vocabulary word in the list above that describes a very dry area of Earth.

Main Idea and Details

Reading Skill

Remember that the *main idea* is what a paragraph is mostly about. Writers often include a topic sentence at the beginning or end of a paragraph. As you read the section "Oceans and Mountains" on page 13, underline the main idea and number the supporting details.

Different Areas of California

The land of California is varied and can be divided into different regions. A **region** is a large area in which places share similar features. California's four major regions are the coast region, the mountain region, the valley region, and the desert region. As you cross California's regions, you will see many landforms. A **landform** is a natural feature of Earth's surface, such as a mountain or hill. Another landform is a valley—the long, low land between hills or mountains.

In California's regions, you will also find different climates. Because of their varied climates, each region has different types of plants and animals.

1. Main Idea and Details **Complete the chart below. Write details about California's regions.**

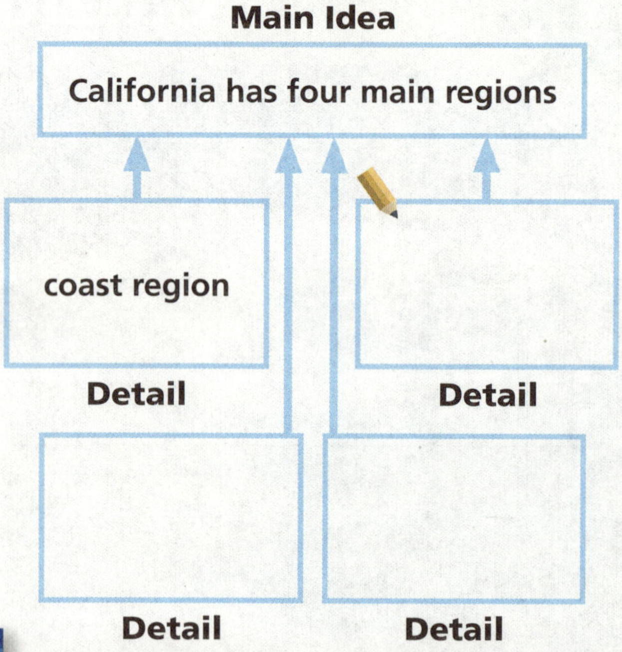

Outline the coast region.

Some areas of California's coast, such as Big Sur, are rocky.

California's state capital was moved to Sacramento in 1854.

California's Capital

Have you ever visited Sacramento, California's state capital? A **capital** is a city where a country's or state's central government is located. A state capital is often near the center of a state. This makes it easier for people from all regions of the state to reach it. Sacramento lies in the Central Valley, in the north-central part of the state.

Ocean and Mountains

Our state's four regions vary greatly in their landforms. California has a very long **coast,** which is the land along an ocean. This shoreline is called the Pacific coast because it lies next to the Pacific Ocean. Southern California's coast features many wide, sandy beaches. Mountain ranges line much of the northern coast. Towering redwood trees grow there too. Near the eastern edge of the state is the Sierra Nevada, a high, snow-covered mountain range.

2. Main Idea and Details
What details in the text help you locate Sacramento?

3. In what way is the northern coast different from the southern coast?
Compare and Contrast

Valleys and Dry Land

Some areas of California are flat and low. The valley region is a flat area of land stretching for miles between the Coast Ranges and the Sierra Nevada. Many farms are located in the valley. The Mojave (moh HAH vee) Desert lies in the southern part of the state. A **desert** is a dry area that gets less than ten inches of rain in a year. Many different kinds of plants, such as creosote bushes and sagebrush, grow in the Mojave Desert.

4. How is the desert region different from the valley region? *Compare and Contrast*

California Elevations

Circle the areas of California that have a lower elevation than the rest of the state.

Death Valley in the Mojave Desert is the lowest point in the Western Hemisphere.

Different Regions and Industries

Each of California's regions has a different environment, including climate, plant life, and landforms. Each region has its own industries, or businesses, that produce things or provide services. People who live there have different types of jobs. One industry that is important throughout the state is tourism. Tourism is the business of providing services to visitors. Many tourists enjoy visiting our state's beaches on the coast, redwood forests, and mountains. Others take in the sights and activities in our large cities.

5. How does the physical environment of a region affect the people who live there? *Cause and Effect*

California's varied tourist attractions include zoos and museums, natural areas, historic sites, and cities.

Coast and Mountain Industries

The state's coast region provides resources for many kinds of jobs. The region's fishing industry supplies fresh fish to restaurants and grocery stores. Many of the state's valuable oil wells are along the southern coast, from Santa Barbara to Long Beach. San Francisco Bay and San Diego Bay form excellent natural harbors. Millions of tons of goods are shipped in and out of these harbors and other California ports every year.

The industries of the mountain region are centered around its forests and minerals. Its trees are used for timber. Timber is wood that is used to make other products. The state's most important timber tree is the Douglas fir. The western side of the Sierra Nevada has gold mines and other resources.

Valley Region Industries

California's valley region is one of the world's best farming areas. Many features, such as rich soil, make the valley well suited for growing crops. The Central Valley is divided into the San Joaquin (wah KEEN) Valley in the south and the Sacramento Valley in the north. These valleys also have rivers that serve as a source of water for the fields. The many fruits and vegetables grown in this area include grapes, tomatoes, and lettuce. All of this farming provides crops for the canning industry.

6. Where in California might you find businesses that repair ships?

Draw Conclusions

Sunflowers are one of the many crops grown in California's Central Valley.

7. Why is the Central Valley an important farming area?

Cause and Effect

The All-American Canal, seen here near Holtville, brings water to farms in the Imperial Valley.

Desert Region Industries

The desert region is rich in minerals—metals and other materials that are dug from the earth. Sand, gravel, and stone are just some of the many minerals found in the desert region. Mining those minerals is a big industry in this region.

Part of the desert region, called the Imperial Valley, has rich soil that gets water from the All-American Canal. The canal brings water from the Colorado River to farms in the Imperial Valley. It provides enough water to make this desert land productive.

8. Why do you think the All-American Canal is important to the Imperial Valley?
Draw Conclusions

Summary

The four regions of California have unique climates, landforms, and industries. Describe the region where you live.

Skill

Map Legends and Map Scales

Learn More A map legend and map scale help you read a map. A legend explains the different symbols on a map. The symbols are the lines, colors, and small drawings that stand for other things. A scale tells what a certain small distance on a map equals in miles and kilometers. To find distances on a map, take a piece of paper and line up the edge from one city to another. Make marks on the edge of the paper to show the locations of the two cities. Now lay the paper along the map scale. That will tell you about how far apart the cities are.

Try It

Use the map to plan a family trip from Los Angeles to Sacramento.

1. **How many miles will you travel on your trip?** Apply

   ____

2. **If your family promised to pick up a relative in Bakersfield on the way, what highways would you take?** Apply

   ____

3. **What symbol tells you that Sacramento is the state capital?** Identify

   ____

California Interstates and Highways

Name:

H-SS 4.1.4 Identify the locations of the Pacific Ocean, rivers, valleys, and mountain passes and explain their effects on the growth of towns.

Lesson 4

How have California's landforms and water affected settlement?

CONNECT TO YOU If you wanted to choose a new place to live, what things would you look for in a new location? When people hundreds of years ago came to what is now California, they usually chose where to live based on several different things. What helped people decide where to live?

Preview the Lesson

Vocabulary

border *(n.)* an official line that separates one place from another

settle *(v.)* to move to and set up a new place to live

mountain pass *(n.)* a narrow gap in a mountain range

natural resource *(n.)* a useful material that comes from the earth

Vocabulary Activity Circle the vocabulary word above that names a landform.

Reading: Cause and Effect

Looking for cause-and-effect relationships helps show how events are related. A *cause* is what makes something happen. An *effect* is what happens as a result of a cause. As you read the lesson, underline cause-and-effect signal words such as *because* and *therefore.*

The Pacific Ocean

Many people who have come to this area have wanted to be close to oceans or rivers for travel. The Pacific Ocean forms the entire western border of California. A **border** is an official line that separates one place from another. In the past, people used the ocean like a highway. They sailed the coast looking for places to settle. To **settle** means to move to and set up a new place to live. The first European settlements, or towns, in California were formed along the Pacific coast.

Across the Mountains

Some of the first explorers came here directly by sea, but by the 1700s, people were coming to the area by land. Settlers from Mexico traveled north to California. In the 1800s, settlers came from the East by following difficult trails. They had to find mountain passes to get across the Sierra Nevada. A **mountain pass** is a narrow gap in a mountain range. Sometimes these mountain passes were named for people who passed through them. The Beckwourth Pass is named for James Beckwourth, a guide who helped people cross the Sierra Nevada. The Donner Pass is named for Jacob Donner, the leader of the Donner party who traveled through this pass.

1. How did the Pacific Ocean affect settlement in California? *Cause and Effect*

2. Main Idea and Details
In the text, circle the names of two mountain passes that settlers used to get to California.

California Mountain Passes

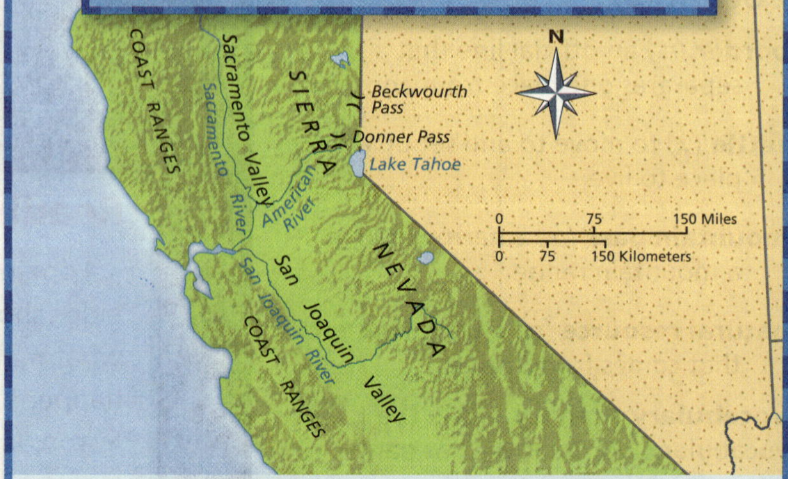

Trace the river that leads from the Donner Pass to the West Coast of California.

People began growing oranges in California's Central Valley in the 1800s.

The Population Grows

Resources were also very important to settlers. **Natural resources** are useful materials that come from the earth, such as food, water, or materials for shelter. California's climates and landforms are varied, and people settled in different areas around the state. Many settlers made it across the mountains to the wide, flat Sacramento and San Joaquin Valleys, which are part of the valley region. These valleys have good soil and receive water from the American, Sacramento, and San Joaquin Rivers. Many people have stayed in this region because it has good conditions for farming.

Resources have also affected how people settled in other regions. With all the resources of the Pacific Ocean, parts of California's coastline became heavily populated. Major cities, such as San Francisco and Los Angeles, became busy trading ports, or places where ships loaded and unloaded goods. The regions with harsh climates are less populated. Therefore, there are fewer communities in the mountains than on the coast. Even fewer people live in the hot, dry Mojave Desert.

3. What caused people to settle in the Sacramento and San Joaquin Valleys rather than in other areas? *Cause and Effect*

Summary

There are several different reasons why people have chosen to settle in certain places in California. List three of those reasons and then pick the one you think would be most important to settlers. Explain your answer.

Primary Source

Photographs

Learn More One way we can learn about the past is by looking at photographs. Photographs are a primary source because they were taken at the time an event happened.

Look at the two photographs below. The first photograph shows families traveling west by covered wagon in the 1800s. The second photograph shows a modern family getting ready to take a journey.

After looking at the photographs, answer the questions below.

1. **In the first photograph, circle two things you would probably not see on a road today. In the second photograph, circle two things people did not have in the 1800s.** *Identify*

2. **What do you think is the biggest difference between traveling to California in the 1800s and today?** *Analyze*

____

____

Name:

H-SS 4.1.5 Use maps, charts, and pictures to describe how communities in California vary in land use, vegetation, wildlife, climate, population density, architecture, services, and transportation.

Lesson 5

How are California's communities alike and different?

CONNECT TO YOU You have learned how the regions in our state are different. Communities in these regions are alike and different in many ways. How would you describe your community to a friend who lives in another part of the state?

Preview the Lesson

Vocabulary

urban area *(n.)* a city area

suburban area *(n.)* an area just outside a city

rural area *(n.)* an area of small towns or farms

agriculture *(n.)* the growing of crops and raising of animals

architecture *(n.)* the style and design of a building

transportation *(n.)* the moving of goods, people, or animals from one place to another

population density *(n.)* the average number of people living in a specific unit of area

Vocabulary Activity Circle the three words above that describe the areas where people might live.

Reading: Compare and Contrast

When you *compare* two or more things, you look for similarities. When you *contrast* them, you look for differences. As you read the last section on page 27, circle the sentences that tell you how the buildings in California's communities are different from one another.

California's Communities

Most people in California live in one of three types of communities. Many Californians live in urban communities, such as Los Angeles and San Francisco. An **urban area** describes a city area. Suburban communities, like Pasadena and Daly City, surround the cities. A **suburban area** refers to an area just outside a city. Not everyone in California lives in or around cities though. Some people live in rural communities. A **rural area** is an area of small towns or farms. The Sacramento and San Joaquin Valleys have many rural communities.

1. How are urban, suburban, and rural communities alike and different?

Compare and Contrast

____

____

____

____

____

Different Environments

Many rural communities in California are centered around **agriculture,** which is the growing of crops and raising of animals. Modesto began as a small agricultural town in the San Joaquin Valley in 1870, but it has grown since then. In the mountains near Lake Tahoe, trees are sometimes made into timber and used to make other products. If you go to Northern California, you will find Eureka, a small city near forests and the ocean. Because of its location, Eureka's important business activities are timber and fishing.

A community such as Blythe, which is located in the desert region, has different natural vegetation than other areas of California. The plants that grow there, such as cactuses, are suited for dry, hot conditions. Desert wildlife includes such animals as coyotes and lizards.

High in the Sierra Nevada, small towns may be found among huge trees, such as redwoods and Douglas firs. Many animals, such as bears, deer, and mountain lions, have made their homes in the mountains.

2. How are the wildlife and vegetation near Blythe different from those near Eureka? *Compare and Contrast*

Vegetation in the desert needs little water in order to grow.

California Resources

Circle a town in a desert region.

California's Climates

California has many different landforms and climates. Along the southern coast, the summers are warm and sunny, and the winters are mild. The northern coast has cooler summers and winters. Areas near the Sacramento and San Joaquin Valleys usually have hot, dry summers and cold, humid winters. In the mountain region, the summers are mild, and it rains during the winter.

Higher up in the mountains, there is plenty of snow. The desert has hot, dry days all year long, but the nights are often cool. In the winter, the desert temperature at night can reach below 0°F. Did you know that the highest temperature ever recorded in the United States were in California's Death Valley? One day in 1913, the temperature reached 134°F (57°C)!

3. Describe the climate of the mountain region.
Main Idea and Details

Recreation in California

There is much to see and do in California. You can visit museums, zoos, and amusement parks. You can go camping, hiking, horseback riding, or bicycling in one of our many local, state, or national parks.

4. Why are there so many different recreational activities in California?
Draw Conclusions

People enjoy camping in California's mountain region.

Many people fish and swim in our lakes and rivers, or along our long coast. Yosemite National Park is a popular place to visit. Here you can see giant sequoias. In the Mojave Desert, many people visit the Joshua Tree National Park. The Joshua tree is not really a tree. It is a type of plant that can grow to be forty feet tall and hundreds of years old.

Living in Communities

Sometimes communities in different parts of the state have different kinds of architecture. **Architecture** is the style and design of a building. Many buildings in Santa Barbara have red tile roofs and adobe, or heavy dried clay, walls. They are built in a Spanish style of architecture because settlers from Spain played an important role in Santa Barbara's early history.

Some of the largest cities, such as San Francisco, Los Angeles, and San Diego, have downtown areas with tall, glass and steel skyscrapers, and large highway systems. San Francisco was built on steep hills and has several transportation systems that are designed to carry people all over the urban and suburban area. **Transportation** refers to the moving of goods, people, or animals from one place to another. One way to travel in San Francisco is by cable car. Cable cars, cars, and buses take people up and down the city's hills. Train systems carry people on above-ground and underground trains. Ferries and bridges help people travel across the San Francisco Bay to nearby urban or suburban areas.

5. Underline the different ways to travel in California's communities.
Compare and Contrast

These buildings in Santa Barbara show a Spanish style of architecture.

Summary

Just as the geography of California is varied, so are the different communities found in the state. Explain how communities are different from one another.

Skill

Population Density Maps

Learn More **Population density** is the average number of people living in a specific unit of area. It is usually measured by how many people live in one square mile. According to the U.S. Census Bureau, California had a population density of 217 people per square mile in 2000. The rest of the United States had an average of only 79 people per square mile. This does not mean that every square mile of California had 217 people. Los Angeles County had an average of 2,344 people living in every square mile. A less populated county, such as Glenn County, had an average of 20 people per square mile. In fact, some counties in the desert region have a population density of fewer than five people per square mile.

Try It

Study the map and then answer the questions below.

1. Circle the areas of California that are most densely populated. How many people are there per square mile in those areas? *Identify*

____

2. Using direction words, tell which areas of California have the fewest people per square mile. *Apply*

____

____

____

Population Density by County

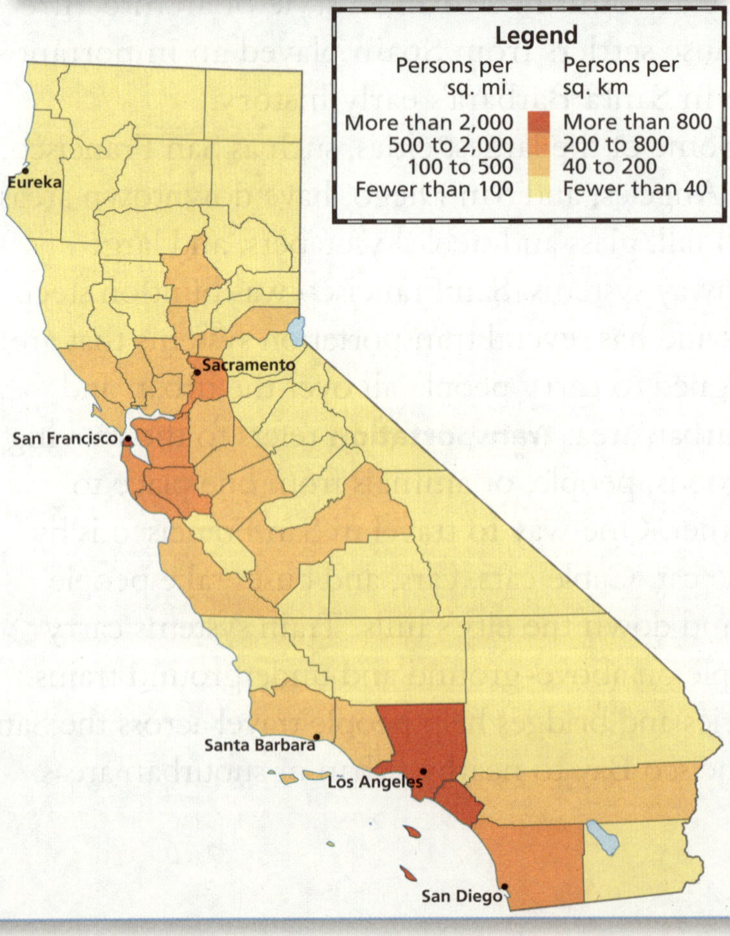

Name:

Unit 2

Study Journal

In this unit you will learn how the arrival of the Spanish changed the lives of the California Indians. You will also learn how life in California changed when Mexico took over the area. Complete the activities on these pages as you read the unit.

What I know about . . .

people who lived in this area hundreds of years ago:

How did Europeans affect life in California?

For each topic below, record information about what the Spanish and Mexicans did. Then tell what effect their actions had on California and the California Indians.

Explorations	Missions	Ranchos
Effect	Effect	Effect

Complete these sections as you read the unit.

Circle the person below who you would like to have joined on his travels. On the lines at the right, describe what you might have seen on your journey.

- **James Cook**
- **Vitus Bering**
- **Juan Cabrillo**
- **Juan Crespi**
- **Junípero Serra**
- **Gaspar de Portolá**
- **Francis Drake**
- **José Figueroa**
- **Father Hidalgo**
- **Juan Bautista de Anza**

Complete the missing information in the time line below.

1600		1800	1900
1602	**1767** Gaspar De Portolá is sent to run the California colony.	**1821**	

I have learned . . .

Name:

H-SS 4.2.1 Discuss the major nations of California Indians, including their geographic distribution, economic activities, legends, and religious beliefs; and describe how they depended on, adapted to, and modified the physical environment by cultivation of land and use of sea resources.

Lesson 1

How did early people live in California?

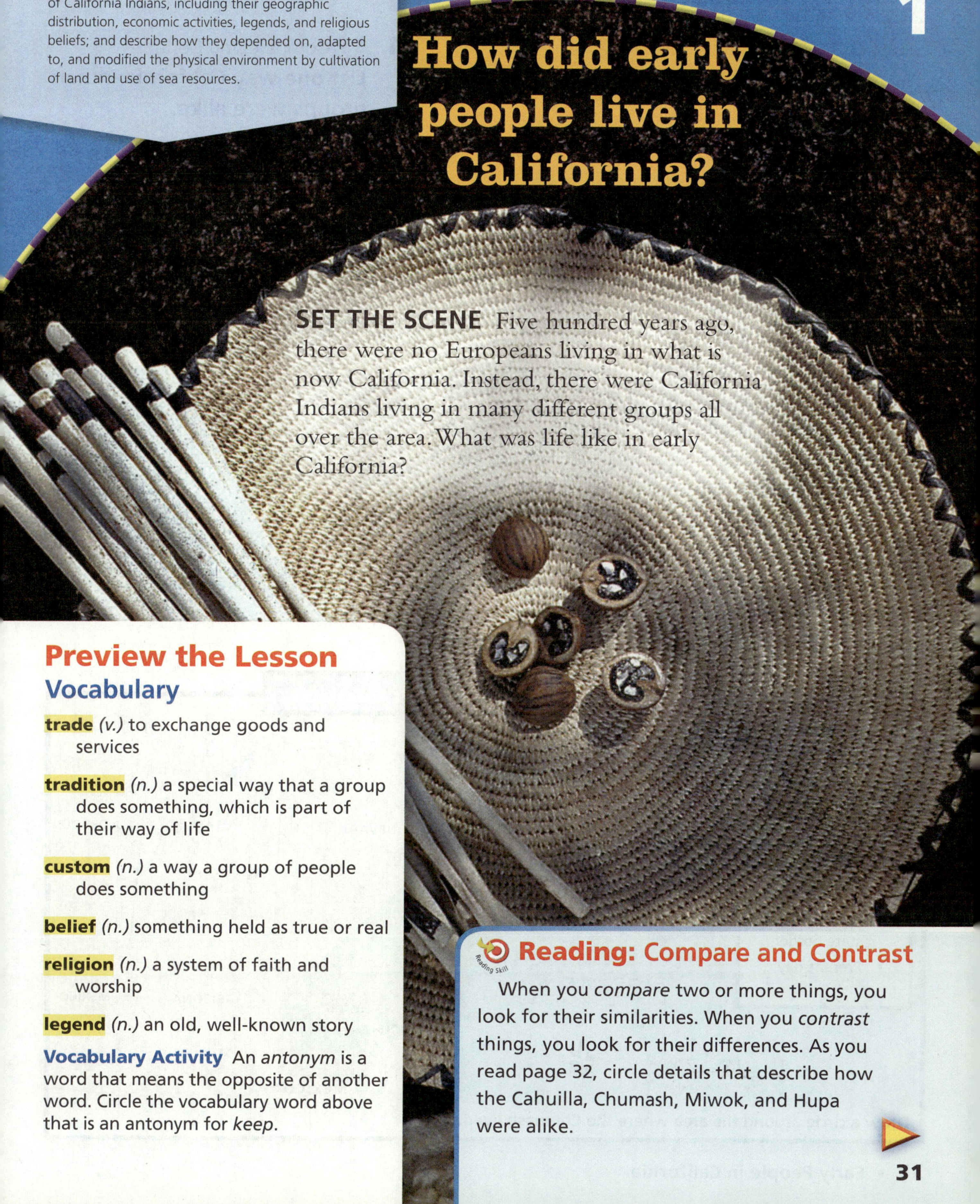

SET THE SCENE Five hundred years ago, there were no Europeans living in what is now California. Instead, there were California Indians living in many different groups all over the area. What was life like in early California?

Preview the Lesson

Vocabulary

trade *(v.)* to exchange goods and services

tradition *(n.)* a special way that a group does something, which is part of their way of life

custom *(n.)* a way a group of people does something

belief *(n.)* something held as true or real

religion *(n.)* a system of faith and worship

legend *(n.)* an old, well-known story

Vocabulary Activity An *antonym* is a word that means the opposite of another word. Circle the vocabulary word above that is an antonym for *keep*.

Reading: Compare and Contrast

Reading Skill

When you *compare* two or more things, you look for their similarities. When you *contrast* things, you look for their differences. As you read page 32, circle details that describe how the Cahuilla, Chumash, Miwok, and Hupa were alike.

California Indian Groups

Many American Indian groups have lived and still live in what is now California. Many archaeologists have learned about the history of California Indians by studying their artifacts, or objects that were made by people long ago. Archaeologists are scientists who study how people lived in the past.

Archaeologists have learned that most of California's Indian groups used the natural resources in their area to survive. For example, most California Indians wove grasses, roots, and bushes into baskets and mats. Trees were used to build homes and boats. Animal bones were used to make tools. If groups ended up with more of these items than they needed, they might have traded them with other groups. To **trade** something is to exchange goods and services. Trade allowed California Indian groups to use a variety of different tools and foods.

1. Compare and Contrast **List one way California Indian groups were alike.**

___

___

___

___

Four California Indian Groups

Draw a circle around the area where the Chumash lived.

The Cahuilla and the Chumash

The Cahuilla (kuh WEE uh) lived near what is now called the Mojave Desert. They hunted antelope and small animals. They lived in a type of reed house called a kish. The Cahuilla women had a tradition of basket weaving. A **tradition** is a special way that a group does something, which is part of their way of life. The baskets were used to store food and water. It was also a tradition for Cahuilla men to sing what are now called "bird songs." These songs told stories about the Cahuilla people.

The Chumash (CHOO mash) mainly lived along the south-central part of California's Pacific coast, near what are now the cities of Santa Barbara and Los Angeles. They ate acorns, fish, shellfish, whales, and sea birds. They also hunted deer and small animals. Chumash traditions included a great respect for large, powerful birds called condors. Chumash houses were shaped like domes and covered with woven grass. Because they lived near the ocean, the Chumash made tools from whalebone and used clam shells as money when trading.

2. Compare and Contrast **Name one way that the Cahuilla and the Chumash were different.**

A Chumash basket

The Chumash used many natural materials to make instruments such as these rattles.

The Miwok and the Hupa

Most of the Miwok (MEE wok) lived near the Sierra Nevada. In the winter, they lived in dirt-covered houses that were built halfway underground for warmth. In the summer, they lived in bark houses above the ground to keep cool. Some Miwok lived along the Pacific coast near what is now San Francisco. They fished and hunted deer. The Miwok had a custom of using holes in slabs of stone to grind acorns into flour. A **custom** is a way a group of people does something.

The Hupa (HOO pah) lived in Northern California's Coast Ranges, near the present-day Oregon border. They hunted elk and deer, and they fished for salmon, trout, and sturgeon. Acorns were another important source of food. One Hupa custom was to build their rectangular homes out of cedar-wood planks. The houses were about twenty feet long. Their bottom halves were built underground.

3. Compare and Contrast
How were the houses built by the Miwok different from those built by the Hupa?

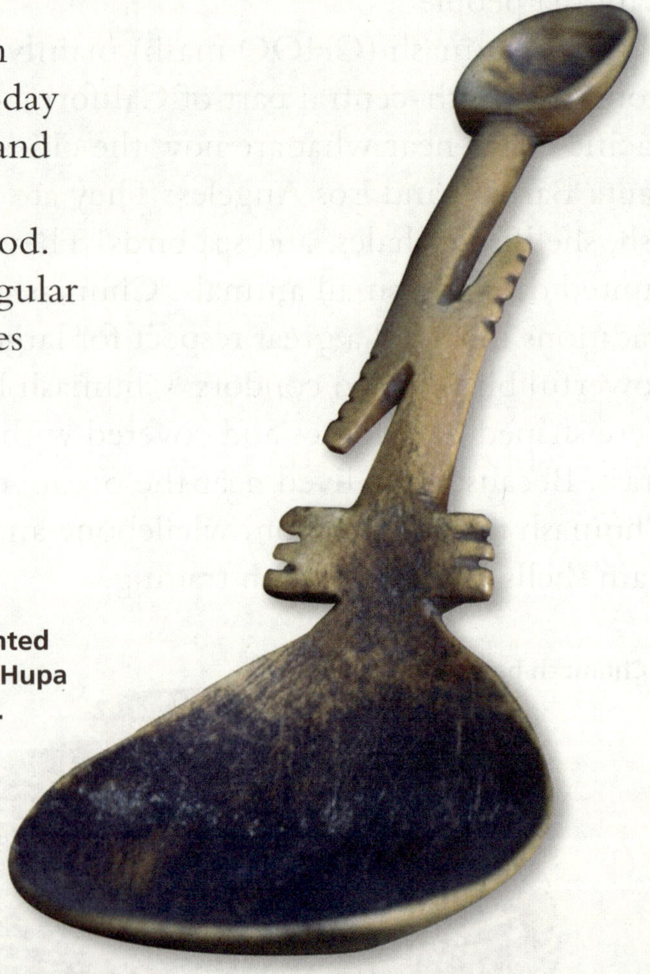

Evidence that the Hupa hunted animals can be seen in this Hupa spoon made from an antler.

Miwok ceremonies are still performed today.

Ceremonies and Stories

Thousands of California Indians live in our state today. Many still honor the **beliefs,** or things held as true or real, of their people. Some of these beliefs have been a part of their **religion,** which is a system of faith and worship, for hundreds of years. Many Chumash believed in three worlds. They believed that an eagle lives in the upper world, humans live in the middle world, and two serpents live in the lower world and hold up the middle world.

Ceremonies have played a large part in many California Indian beliefs. The Hupa held ceremonies for the purpose of preventing earthquakes, floods, or crop failures. In some Miwok ceremonies, people still dance in costumes made from animal skins and feathers.

California Indians often pass along their traditions and beliefs through **legends,** or old, well-known stories. A myth is a story that explains something. One Cahuilla myth tells about twin brothers who created the world.

4. Write the California Indian group name under its belief or custom. *Main Idea and Details*

a. Held ceremonies to prevent earthquakes

____

b. Believed in three worlds

____

c. Dance in costumes made from animal skins and feathers

____

d. Have a myth about twin brothers

____

Summary

California Indian groups have many customs, traditions, and beliefs. In what ways were the lives of these groups connected to the land and its resources?

Skill

Matrices

Learn More A matrix is a kind of chart. It is one way to show and compare information. A matrix groups information under headings across the top of the chart. It also groups the information in another way along the left side of the matrix.

The matrix below lists facts about four groups of California Indians. Read the headings along both the top and left side of the chart. To find information about a group, locate the name of that group at the top. Then run your finger down the column to read about the group's region, foods, homes, and customs.

	Chumash	Cahuilla	Miwok	Hupa
Region	central part of coast	near Mojave Desert	near Sierra Nevada	in North Coast Ranges
Foods	acorns, deer, fish, whales	antelope and small animals	deer, fish, acorns	deer, fish, acorns
Homes	dome-shaped, covered with woven grass		in winter, half underground, covered with dirt; in summer, bark houses	made from cedar planks
Customs and Traditions	used clam shells for trading	men sang songs now called "bird songs"	danced in costumes made from animal skins	basket weaving

Try It

1. **Fill in the missing information in the matrix about the homes of the Cahuilla.** *Identify*
2. **Underline the area where the Chumash lived.** *Identify*
3. **Draw a star next to the names of the groups who ate similar foods.** *Analyze*
4. **What is one way that the Chumash are different from the Hupa?** *Interpret*

____

____

Name:

H-SS 4.2.2 Identify the early land and sea routes to, and European settlements in, California with a focus on the exploration of the North Pacific (e.g., by Captain James Cook, Vitus Bering, Juan Cabrillo), noting especially the importance of mountains, deserts, ocean currents, and wind patterns.

Lesson 2

How did early Europeans come to California?

SET THE SCENE When people come to a place they have never seen, they often look around to learn more about it. In the 1500s, European countries wanted to learn about new places. Who were some of the first Europeans to come to the land that is now California?

Preview the Lesson

Vocabulary

explore *(v.)* to travel to places in order to learn more about them

current *(n.)* the pattern of the flow of water

Vocabulary Activity If the suffix *-er* can mean "one who does something," what might *explorer* mean?

People

Juan Cabrillo
Francis Drake
Vitus Bering
James Cook

Reading: Sequence

Writers organize information in a *sequence* or certain order. Sometimes they use dates to show a sequence. As you read page 38, underline any specific dates that you find.

1550

1600

1542 Juan Cabrillo lands in San Diego Bay.

1579 Sir Francis Drake explores the California coast.

1602 Sebastián Vizcaíno lands in Monterey Bay.

Europeans Come to California

In the 1500s, European countries began sending people across the Atlantic Ocean to explore North and South America. To **explore** means to travel to places in order to learn more about them. In 1542 Spanish explorer Juan Cabrillo sailed north from what is now Mexico to find a route to Asia. He explored present-day San Diego, Cape San Martin, and San Miguel Island. Sailors, soldiers, and enslaved Africans went with him. The Spanish named this area Alta California, meaning "Upper California." They often just called it "California."

Many explorers came after Cabrillo. In 1579 English explorer Sir Francis Drake sailed north along California's coast. He found a small bay near present-day San Francisco and named the area Nova (New) Albion. Albion was an older name for the island of England. In 1602 Spanish explorer Sebastián Vizcaíno explored the area from present-day San Diego to present-day Monterey. He made maps of the coast that were used by other explorers until the late 1700s.

Some explorers came to this area from a different direction. Vitus Bering traveled northeast from Russia across the Pacific Ocean. In 1728 he found a water route between Russia and present-day Alaska. This passage was later named the Bering Strait. In the late 1700s and early 1800s, Russian traders took Bering's route and came to California from the north.

1. Use information from the time line and the text to number the explorers in the order in which they explored California. Sequence

___ **Francis Drake**

___ **Juan Cabrillo**

___ **Sebastián Vizcaíno**

Voyages to California

On the map, draw an arrow that shows the direction Cabrillo traveled.

1778

Captain James Cook is pictured here speaking with a group of American Indians. He explored the Pacific Northwest in 1778.

Challenges of Exploring

The California coast was not an easy place to explore. Sailors had to deal with strong winds and ocean currents that carried their ships off course. A **current** is the pattern of the flow of water. Also, the rocky coastline made it difficult to find a safe place to harbor a ship.

Once explorers reached land, it was hard to travel inland because of the Coast Ranges. After many months at sea, most explorers did not want to cross mountains.

Explorers found that different areas of California had very different climates. The area west of the Coast Ranges is foggy and mild. If explorers made it over the mountains in Southern California, they found themselves in a desert.

2. Circle details in the text that describe why California was a difficult place to explore.
Main Idea and Details

Summary

Exploring California was difficult, but Europeans continued to come to the area and learn more about it. What were the major challenges for people exploring California?

Biography

James Cook, 1728–1779

Learn More Growing up in Britain, James Cook was a smart and curious student. He became an apprentice to both a store owner and a shipowner as a young man. An apprentice is someone who learns a skill or a trade from someone else. It was during these years that Cook became interested in the sea.

Cook became a well-known sailor, explorer, and mapmaker. He joined Britain's Royal Navy. Cook mapped the coastlines of New Zealand and eastern Australia while sailing on a ship called the *Endeavour.* He later explored the seas around Antarctica on a ship called the *Resolution.* His final voyage was also on the *Resolution.* Cook searched for the Northwest Passage, a route that connects the Atlantic and Pacific Oceans. He never found this route, but his travels led him to explore the West Coast of North America from present-day Oregon to the Bering Strait.

1. **Underline the sentence that describes something Cook did as an explorer. Circle the sentence that describes something he did as a mapmaker.** *Identify*
2. **Why do you think a sailor might be a good mapmaker?** *Analyze*

____

____

____

____

____

Name:

H-SS 4.2.3 Describe the Spanish exploration and colonization of California, including the relationships among soldiers, missionaries, and Indians (e.g., Juan Crespi, Junipero Serra, Gaspar de Portola).

Lesson 3

How did the Spanish change how California Indians lived?

SET THE SCENE In the 1700s, more Europeans were exploring and settling in California. At this time, there were already hundreds of thousands of California Indians living in the area. How did Spanish settlement affect how the California Indians lived?

Preview the Lesson

Vocabulary

colony *(n.)* a settlement of people who come from one country to live in another land

expedition *(n.)* a journey made for a special purpose

missionary *(n.)* a person who teaches his or her religion to people who have different beliefs

mission *(n.)* a settlement set up by a religious group to teach their religion and other ways of life to native people

Catholicism *(n.)* the religion of the Catholic Church

Vocabulary Activity Which of the vocabulary words above is also part of another word on the list? Draw a line connecting the two words.

People

Gaspar de Portolá
Juan Bautista de Anza
Juan Crespi
Junípero Serra

Reading: Compare and Contrast

When you *compare* two or more things, you look for similarities. When you *contrast,* you look for differences. As you read about the different Spanish people who arrived in California, underline the reasons why they came.

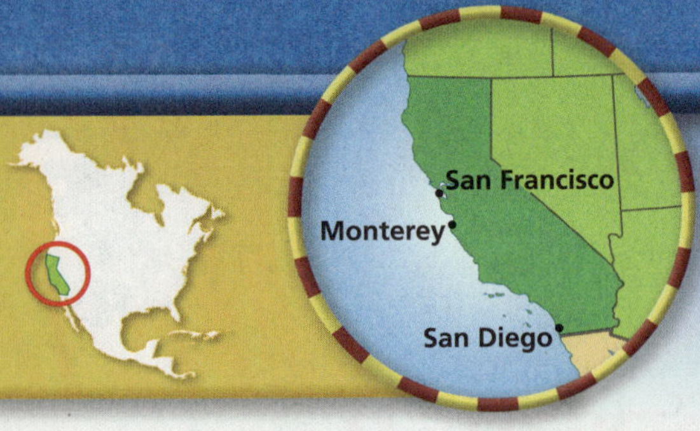

1767

1767

1769

1769 Father Serra starts the San Diego mission.

Europeans Settle in California

In 1767 Spain sent a soldier named Gaspar de Portolá to run its California colony. A **colony** is a settlement of people who come from one country to live in another land. When he arrived in California, Portolá led an expedition to explore the area near present-day Monterey. An **expedition** is a journey made for a special purpose.

Two Spanish missionaries traveled with Portolá's expedition. A **missionary** is a person who teaches his or her religion to people who have different beliefs. Father Juan Crespi kept a journal about the trip. Father Junípero Serra started the mission at San Diego in 1769. A **mission** is a settlement set up by a religious group to teach their religion and other ways of life to native people.

Later, in 1775 Captain Juan Bautista de Anza led an expedition of hundreds of Spanish settlers. They settled in the area that is now San Francisco.

1. Compare and Contrast

How is a mission similar to a colony?

Mission San Luis Rey de Francia was established in 1798.

1771 1773 1775

1775 California Indians destroy the San Diego mission.

California Indians learned new skills on missions. This illustration shows women and children making rope.

Problems at the Missions

The missionaries wanted the California Indians to come to the missions. They gave them gifts such as beads, clothing, and food so they would live in the missions. There these California Indians learned how to farm and make new things.

However, once they came to the missions, some California Indians were not free to leave. They were forced to give up their way of life and work hard. They also had to learn Spanish and follow **Catholicism,** the religion of the Catholic Church. Many died from diseases, such as measles and smallpox, that were brought over by Europeans.

A few California Indians fought against the mission system. Some of this resistance was violent. For example, California Indians destroyed the San Diego mission in 1775. Others never joined a mission. They chose to stay on their lands and keep their ways of life.

2. Name one way that the California Indians resisted the Spanish. *Main Idea and Details*

Summary

The Spanish missionaries wanted the California Indians to live in the missions. How did the missions change the lives of some of the California Indians?

Biography

Junípero Serra, 1713–1784

Learn More When Miguel José Serra was a young man in Majorca, Spain, he decided to become a Franciscan priest in the Catholic Church. He had read many books about missionaries traveling to new places to spread their religion. Serra decided that he wanted to be a missionary. He took Junípero as his religious name, becoming Junípero Serra.

In 1749 Serra left Spain to begin missionary work. After spending some years in Mexico, Serra traveled north to set up missions. Three of these missions were San Diego de Alcalá, San Antonio de Padua, and San Francisco de Asís. Serra established a total of nine missions, all in present-day California. The missions introduced many California Indians to Catholicism. They also helped Spain protect the area from Russian and British settlers.

1. **Circle the names of three missions established by Junípero Serra.** *Identify*
2. **Why did Junípero Serra want to establish missions?** *Analyze*

____

____

____

____

Name:

H-SS 4.2.4 Describe the mapping of, geographic basis of, and economic factors in the placement and function of the Spanish missions; and understand how the mission system expanded the influence of Spain and Catholicism throughout New Spain and Latin America.

Lesson 4

What was Spain's influence in California?

SET THE SCENE If you were going to build a settlement in a new place, wouldn't you want it to be in the right place? When building missions, Spain had to think about where to locate them so that they would be successful. How do you think the success of the Spanish missions in California made Spain's colony stronger?

Preview the Lesson

Vocabulary

fort *(n.)* a building used by soldiers to defend an important place

Vocabulary Activity Draw a line from the word *fort* to the fort shown on this page.

Reading: Cause and Effect

Writers use cause and effect to help readers see connections between events. A *cause* is what makes something happen. An *effect* is what happens as a result. As you read page 46, underline details that tell what caused Spain to build missions in California.

1760

1775

1769 The Spanish build the first California mission at San Diego.

1770

The Location of Missions

Spanish missionaries built many missions in California and throughout Spain's colonies in the Americas. They wanted the California Indians to be Catholic. From 1769 to 1821, many missions were created in California.

The Spanish government wanted the number of Catholic missions in California to grow. This was because California was an important part of Spain's land in North America, which was called New Spain. The Spanish thought that if California Indians believed in Catholicism, they would support Spain's colony.

To attract large numbers of California Indians, the missions had to be built near where the groups lived. The missions were also built near natural resources such as rivers, forests, and fertile land that was good for growing crops.

The Spanish built many missions in California, such as this one in San Diego in 1769.

1. What effect did Spain hope the Catholic missions would have on the California Indians? *Cause and Effect*

Missions in California

Circle the mission that is located in the present-day city of San Diego.

1823 The last California mission, San Francisco Solano, is built at Sonoma.

The missions also had to be safe and easy to get to. They were close to bays on the coast so that ships could land nearby. A trail called El Camino Real was started in 1770 to connect the missions. The Spanish built forts along the trail to serve as military and trading posts. A **fort** is a building used by soldiers to defend an important place.

Most of the missions were built one day's journey from the next mission along El Camino Real.

The Catholic Church in California

The missions' priests were part of a Catholic group known as the Franciscans. They taught the California Indians how to make things such as olive oil and leather goods. Then the missionaries traded these items for products from the eastern United States. At this time, California missions produced goods for trade with other countries. The missions earned money from trading. This made the missions even more important to the Spanish.

Because the missions were important, the priests who ran them gained power. In fact, some priests, such as Father Junípero Serra, were given control over the soldiers in their areas.

2. Why do you think the missionaries taught the California Indians how to make certain products?
Draw Conclusions

Summary

The missions gave Spain more control over California and the rest of New Spain. How was Spain able to do this?

Primary Source

Letters: Father Junípero Serra

Learn More Letters are also an example of a primary source. They can tell us someone's thoughts and give descriptions about events as they are happening. You have already learned that Father Junípero Serra came to San Diego from Spain and started the first mission in California. Below is a passage from a letter he wrote on July 3, 1769. He wrote this letter to Father Palou, who later wrote Serra's biography.

Read the passage and then answer the questions.

1. Circle the words in the passage that describe the geography of the area. *Identify*
2. How might the land, water, grapes, and roses make this a good place to start a mission? *Analyze*

____

____

____

____

____

____

"The tract through which we passed is generally very good land, with plenty of water; and there, as well as here, the country is neither rocky nor overrun with brushwood. There are, however, many hills, but they are composed [made] of earth. . . . About half-way the valleys and banks of rivulets [small rivers] began to be delightful. We found vines of a large size, and in some cases quite loaded with grapes; we also found an abundance of roses, which appeared to be like those of Castile [a large region of north and central Spain]."

Name:

H-SS 4.2.5 Describe the daily lives of the people, native and nonnative, who occupied the presidios, missions, ranchos, and pueblos.

Lesson 5

What was life like in Spanish and Mexican California?

SET THE SCENE People who move to an area for different reasons often live in different kinds of communities. This was true of the Spanish and Mexican settlers who lived in California. How were these new settlements different?

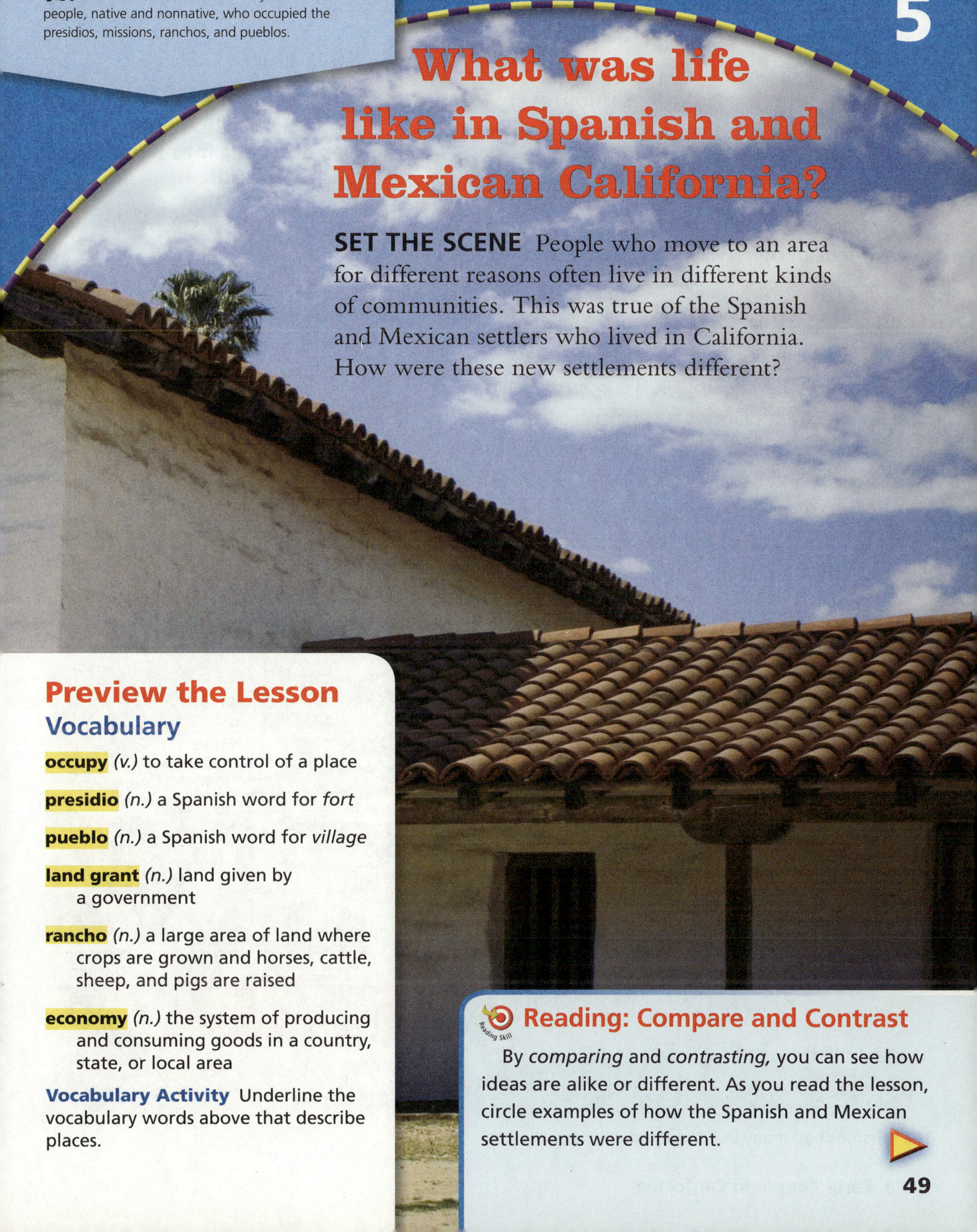

Preview the Lesson

Vocabulary

occupy *(v.)* to take control of a place

presidio *(n.)* a Spanish word for *fort*

pueblo *(n.)* a Spanish word for *village*

land grant *(n.)* land given by a government

rancho *(n.)* a large area of land where crops are grown and horses, cattle, sheep, and pigs are raised

economy *(n.)* the system of producing and consuming goods in a country, state, or local area

Vocabulary Activity Underline the vocabulary words above that describe places.

Reading: Compare and Contrast

Reading Skill

By *comparing* and *contrasting,* you can see how ideas are alike or different. As you read the lesson, circle examples of how the Spanish and Mexican settlements were different.

Missions

As you have learned, the missions were set up mostly for religious purposes. Many California Indians worked on missions. The men farmed and cared for the animals while the women cooked, sewed, gardened, and made candles and soap. Older people fished and made arrows.

Spanish Forts

The Spanish began to occupy areas of California in the late 1600s. To **occupy** means to take control of a place. The Spanish set up presidios to protect the areas they occupied. A **presidio** is a Spanish word for *fort*. Each presidio was home to soldiers who defended the missions as well as any Spanish settlers living in the area. Presidios also became centers for trade.

1. Compare and Contrast **Underline examples of how work on missions was different for men and women.**

2. **What was the purpose of a presidio?** *Main Idea and Details*

A Spanish Mission

The missions had many buildings and work areas.

Farming Villages

The Spanish government also set up pueblos on farmland near the presidios. A **pueblo** is a Spanish word for *village*. People living in the pueblos grew food for soldiers in the presidios. Pueblo workers received money, land, and animals in return for supplying the presidios with food and water.

Mexican Ranches

In 1821 Mexico won its independence from Spain. The Mexican government took over California and gave land grants to Mexicans who were living or moving here. A **land grant** is land given by a government. Many settlers built **ranchos,** or large areas of land where crops are grown and horses, cattle, sheep, and pigs are raised. Ranchos were often used to raise large numbers of livestock while pueblos were mostly used for growing crops. Over time, ranchos replaced missions as the center of the area's economy. An **economy** is the system of producing and consuming goods in a country, state, or local area. Under Mexican rule, raising cattle became an important way for California settlers to make a living.

3. Why were pueblos important to the presidios?

Main Idea and Details

4. Compare and Contrast **Underline examples in the text that show how ranchos and pueblos were different.**

Clay bricks, such as these at El Presidio de Santa Barbara, were dried and then used for building.

Summary

Different kinds of settlements were important to the history of California. Describe the four kinds of settlements that developed during Spanish and Mexican rule.

Skill

Relative Location

Learn More You learned in Unit 1 that every place on Earth has an absolute location. If you are given a place's latitude and longitude, you can find its exact location.

Places also have relative locations. A relative location tells where a place is in relation to some other place. Relative locations are usually given in terms of distance and direction. For example, you could say that San Francisco's relative location is about 400 miles northwest of Los Angeles. Every place has many relative locations. You could also find San Francisco's relative location to Sacramento, San Jose, or any other place.

Try It

1. Use the map to find San Diego's relative location to Sacramento. *Interpret*

   ____

   ____

2. Find San Jose's relative location to Long Beach. *Interpret*

   ____

   ____

3. Which city has a relative location of about 110 miles west of Fresno? *Analyze*

   ____

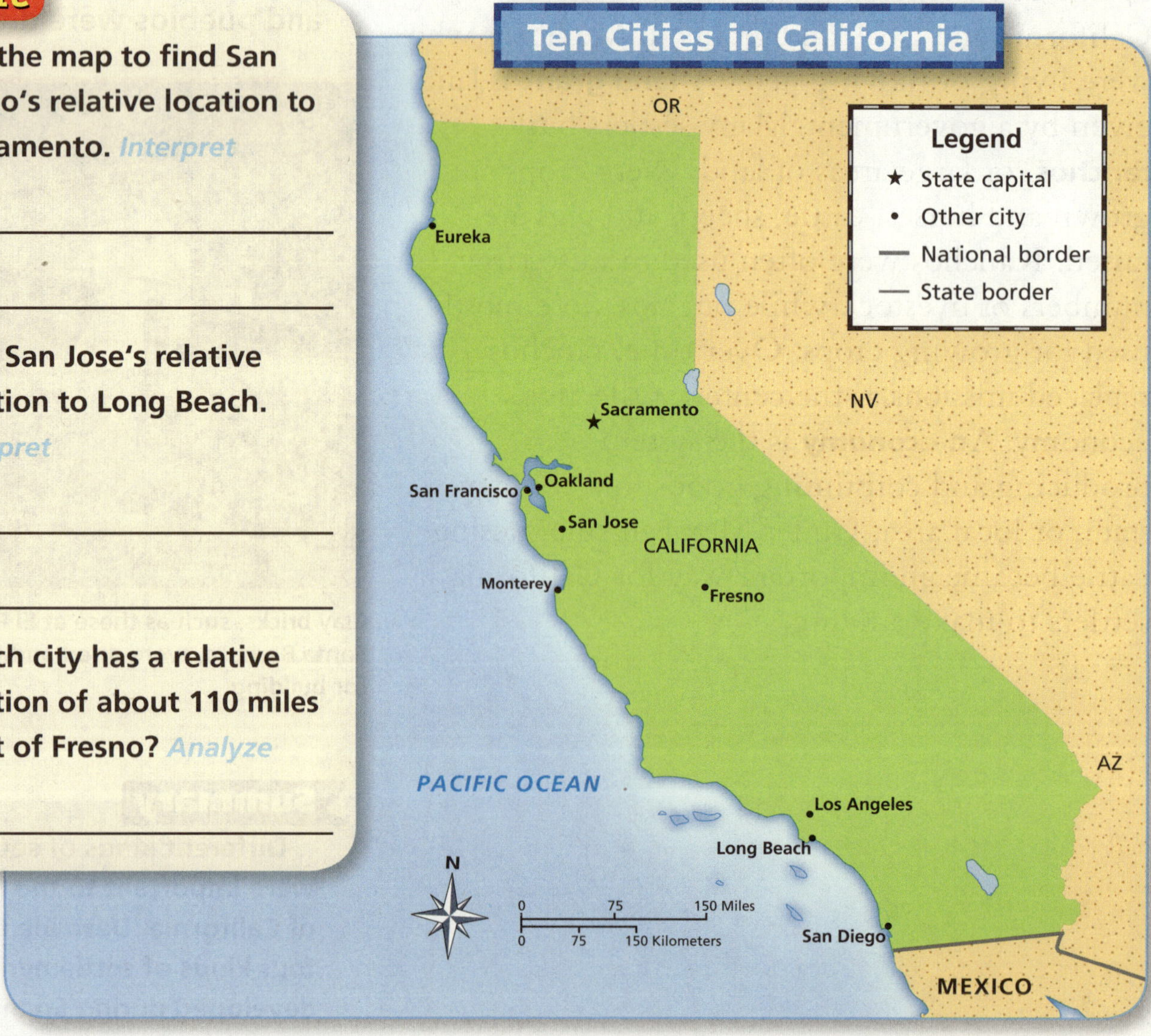

Name:

H-SS 4.2.6 Discuss the role of the Franciscans in changing the economy of California from a hunter-gatherer economy to an agricultural economy.

Lesson 6

How did California's early economy change?

SET THE SCENE Hundreds of years ago, there were no grocery stores or restaurants in California. Most people had to catch or gather their own food. When the Spanish came, they changed the economy of California.

Preview the Lesson

Vocabulary

hunter-gatherer *(n.)* a person who gets food by hunting animals and gathering plants

dam *(n.)* a wall built to hold back water

cultivate *(v.)* to prepare and use land to grow crops

irrigation *(n.)* the use of pipes or ditches to bring water to where it is needed

Vocabulary Activity Three of the vocabulary words above might appear in a story about things farmers do or use to grow crops. Circle those words.

Reading: Compare and Contrast

Reading Skill

To *compare* is to show how two or more things are similar. To *contrast* is to show how they are different. As you read the lesson, circle the sentences that show the differences between how early California Indians used the land before and after the Spanish arrived.

Living off the Land

Before Europeans arrived in California, most California Indians were hunter-gatherers. A **hunter-gatherer** is a person who gets food by hunting animals and gathering plants. The California Indians lived off the animal and plant life that they could find where they lived. They learned about the living things around them, including what was safe to eat and where to find it.

Finding Food

California Indians developed many ways to collect food. They fished and also hunted for sea lions, otters, deer, elk, rabbits, and birds. They gathered acorns, seeds, roots, and berries.

California Indians used different tools to get food. These included pointed sticks, stones, spears, canoes, traps, and woven baskets. They also used bows and arrows to hunt. They even built dams on rivers to gather many fish in one place. A **dam** is a wall built to hold back water.

1. Compare and Contrast **How are the ways the early California Indians found their food different from how people get their food today?**

2. **Why do you think hunter-gatherers developed so many tools?** *Draw Conclusions*

Many California Indians used tools such as arrow heads

The Hupa made dugout canoes using tree trunks.

Missions used stone irrigation ditches to bring water to fields and gardens.

Learning How to Farm

The arrival of the Spanish changed the economy of the California Indians from a hunter-gatherer economy to an agricultural economy. An agricultural economy is based on growing more food than is needed for survival. The extra food can be sold or traded for other goods or services.

Some California Indian groups farmed before the Spanish arrived in California. Most groups lived near streams, the ocean, or forests where wild animals and plants were plentiful.

During the 1700s and 1800s, the Franciscan missionaries taught many California Indians how to cultivate the land. To **cultivate** means to prepare and use land to grow crops. California Indians learned how to grow wheat, corn, and vegetables. These California Indians also learned how to build irrigation systems. **Irrigation** is the use of pipes or ditches to bring water to where it is needed. This system helped them grow more crops in more places.

3. Compare and Contrast **How is a hunter-gatherer economy different from an agricultural economy?**

Summary

When the Spanish came to what is now California, they affected the economy of the California Indians. Describe how an agricultural economy developed in California.

Primary Source

Diaries: Pedro Font

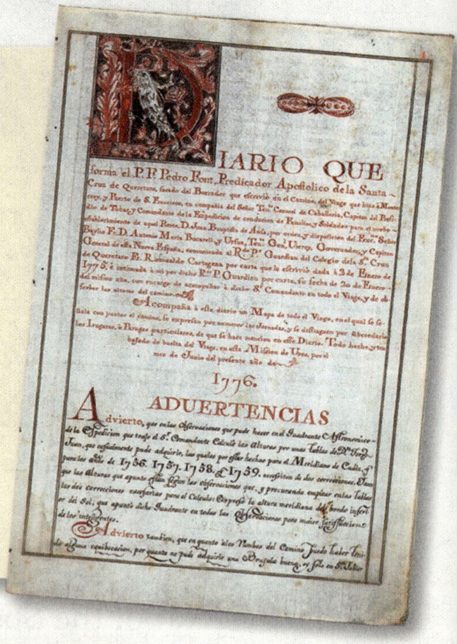

Learn More A diary is also a primary source because it is a record of events written by a person as the events happened. In 1775 a group of Spanish families came north from Mexico. They wanted to settle in the area that is now San Francisco. A priest named Father Pedro Font traveled with them. He kept a diary of the journey. In this passage from his diary, he writes about visiting California Indians who lived near a mission.

November 1, 1775

"[The fields] are . . . on the banks of the river. . . . [The stream] carries so little water that when an Indian waded in and crossed it the water only reached half way up his legs. This is the reason why they had not yet planted . . . for the river was so low that the water could not enter the ditches. And they told me . . . that to remedy this they planned to . . . fasten many logs in the middle of the river, and then many branches, to raise the water so that it would enter the ditches."

Answer the questions below using the diary passage.

1. **The diary explains that the California Indians are planning to build a dam. Circle the words that tell what this dam will be made of.** *Identify*

2. **What do you think was the purpose of the dam?** *Interpret*

____

____

Name:

H-SS 4.2.7 Describe the effects of the Mexican War for Independence on Alta California, including its effects on the territorial boundaries of North America.

Lesson 7

How did the Mexican War for Independence affect California?

SET THE SCENE Have you ever wondered why so many places in California have Spanish names? It's because California was settled and ruled by Spain and then ruled by Mexico. How did Mexico become an independent country and gain control of California?

Preview the Lesson

Vocabulary

government *(n.)* a country's laws and leaders

territory *(n.)* a geographic area that relies on an outside government but usually has some independence

boundary *(n.)* a line or natural feature that separates one area, state, or country from another

Vocabulary Activity Fill in the blank in the sentence below with the correct vocabulary word.

A river forms the ______________ that separated Mexico from the United States.

Reading: Cause and Effect

Being able to find the *causes* of events will help you understand why they happen. As you read, underline important causes that led to the Mexican War for Independence.

1805 1810

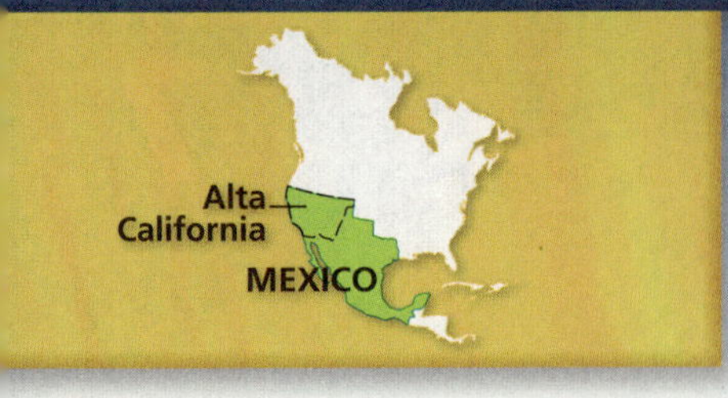

Fighting for Equality

In the early 1800s, many Mexicans in Alta California wanted to be free from Spain. Different groups had different reasons for wanting independence. One group wanted everyone to be treated fairly and equally. This same group wanted to take land away from wealthy landowners and share it with people who had no land. Spain stopped several small fights in Mexico during this time. But the struggle for independence grew.

Landowners Help

Many landowners and others in Mexico also wanted independence from Spain. They saw that Spain's government was becoming more democratic. A **government** is a country's laws and leaders. A democratic government lets its citizens have a say in how the country is run. Some landowners did not want Mexico to become democratic because they thought that they would have to share their land and power. So these landowners helped pay for an army to fight against Spain.

Mexican armies fought for their colony's independence from Spain under flags such as this one.

1. What caused some people to want to take land away from wealthy landowners?
Cause and Effect

2. Why did the wealthy landowners help Mexico's struggle for independence?
Main Ideas and Details

1815 | 1820 | 1825

1821 Mexico wins independence from Spain.

Mexico Wins Independence

Mexico finally won its independence from Spain in 1821 and took over most of Spain's land in North America. This included the territory of Alta California. A **territory** is a geographic area that relies on an outside government but usually has some independence. The boundaries of Alta California outlined the area that is now California, Nevada, Utah, and Arizona. A **boundary** is a line or natural feature that separates one area, state, or country from another.

Shade in the area of the map that represents Alta California.

3. Circle in the text the present-day states that were once part of Alta California.

Main Idea and Details

The Mexican War for Independence came to an end in 1821.

Summary

Different groups of people in Mexico wanted independence from Spain for different reasons. What were two reasons that Mexicans wanted to be free from Spain in the early 1800s?

Citizenship

Celebrating Mexican Independence

Learn More Many citizens in California express their respect for our state's heritage by celebrating Mexican Independence Day. Mexico's move toward independence began on September 16, 1810. At that time, the California territory was a part of Mexico. On that day, Father Hidalgo (ee THAHL go) called for an end to Spain's rule of Mexico. He thought that all people in Mexico should be treated equally, and he wanted it to be possible for everyone to own land. It took eleven years for the Mexican people to win their fight. Finally, on August 24, 1821, Mexico won its freedom from Spain.

Independence Day is celebrated by Mexicans on September 16, the day that Father Hidalgo first demanded freedom for his country. Many Californians from Mexico celebrate this day with parades and picnics.

1. Look at the picture of people celebrating Mexican Independence Day. Circle one thing that you might also see at an American Independence Day celebration on the Fourth of July. *Identify*

2. Draw a box around one person in the picture. What do think this person is feeling? *Analyze*

____

____

____

____

Name:

H-SS 4.2.8 Discuss the period of Mexican rule in California and its attributes, including land grants, secularization of the missions, and the rise of the rancho economy.

Lesson
8

How did Mexican rule affect California?

SET THE SCENE When someone new takes control of something, he or she often makes changes. That is what Mexico did when it took over California. What changes did Mexican rule bring to California, and how did it affect the region and its people?

Preview the Lesson

Vocabulary

tax *(n.)* money the government collects to pay for its services

Vocabulary Activity Write a definition for the word *tax* in your own words.

Reading: Main Idea and Details

A *main idea* states what a paragraph is mostly about. Other sentences include *details* that support the main idea. As you read, underline the main idea of each paragraph in the lesson.

Mexican Rule in California

After winning its independence, Mexico did not want Spain to have any power in California. In 1834 the Mexican governor of California, José Figueroa (fee gay ROH ah), ordered that most of the Spanish missions in California be turned into Mexican settlements. The land of the San Juan Capistrano mission was made into a pueblo and given to California Indians. As a result, the Spanish priests and presidio soldiers lost their power and control over the area.

1. **How did the missions change under Mexican rule?** *Main Ideas and Details*

Free Land and the Rancho Economy

Many Mexican settlers in California received land grants. Between 1821 and 1848, the Mexican government gave out hundreds of land grants. Most of these went to wealthy Californios, or Spanish Mexican settlers, who had connections to the government. The government wanted to give the land to the Californios because then it could collect taxes on the property. A **tax** is money the government collects to pay for its services.

Many new settlers started ranchos. As you have learned, the livestock and crops raised on the ranchos became an important part of California's economy. Under Mexican rule, the California ranchos became powerful and replaced the missions as the centers of government. Rancho owners began to act as the government of their areas.

2. **Why did the ranchos become powerful?** *Draw Conclusions*

Vaqueros, or cowboys, often handled the livestock on California's ranches.

Today, visitors can see what life was like on a California rancho at Petaluma Adobe State Historic Park.

Effects on California Indians

Mexican rule brought some changes for the California Indians. Many of the California Indians who lived on the missions were told they could leave the missions. They were also promised some of the mission land. But most of the land went to the Californios, not to the California Indians. Many California Indians had no land or money, so they lived and worked on the ranchos, just as they had worked at the missions.

3. What effect did Mexican rule have on the California Indians? *Cause and Effect*

Summary

When Mexico took over control of California, the government made changes. Who benefited the most from Mexican rule in California? Explain your answer.

Primary Source

Historical Maps: Land Grants

Learn More In 1848 California became part of the United States. While controlled by the United States, California continued the system of land grants. One way people knew the boundaries of their land grant was by making a map. Maps could be used as official documents showing the land owned by a family or organization.

The map below is a land grant for a Sonoma County rancho. Maps like this one are primary sources. They show the locations of plots of land and tell who owned them at that time.

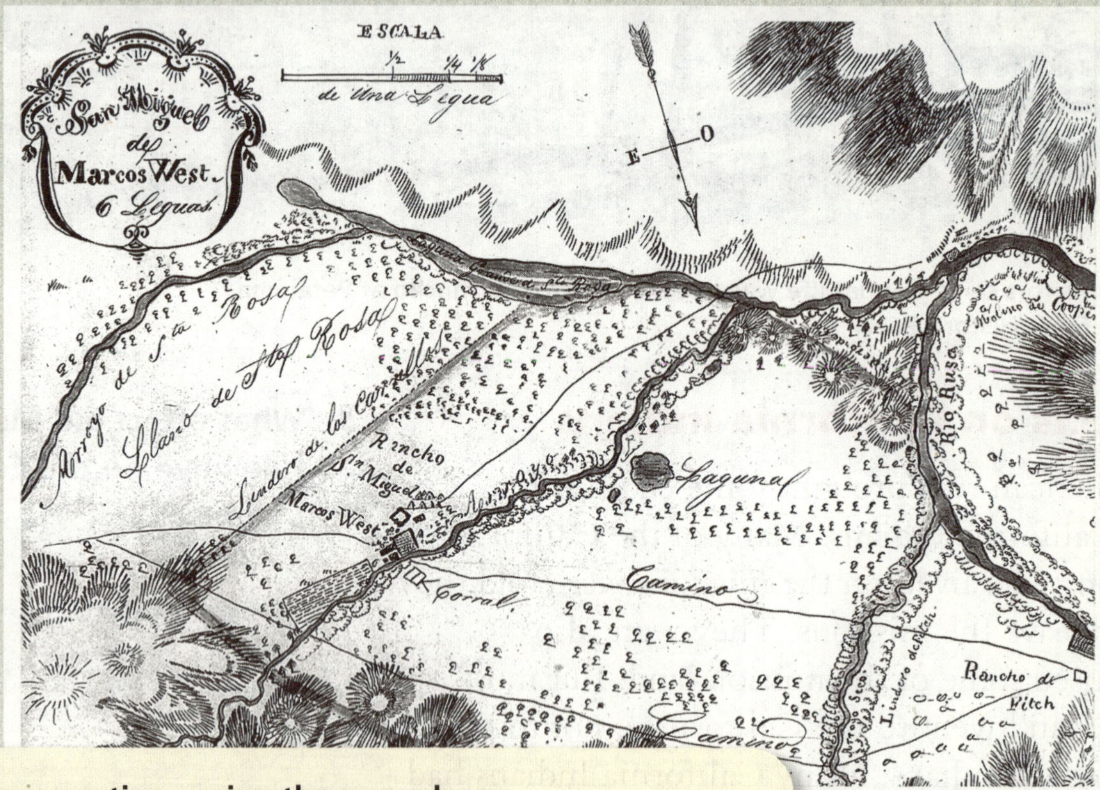

Answer the questions using the map above.

1. **Circle the map scale on the map.** *Identify*

2. **Why would it be important for a rancho owner to have a map like this?** *Analyze*

____

____

Name:

Unit 3

Study Journal

In this unit you will learn how California went from a Spanish colony to part of the United States. You will see how the California Gold Rush brought new people to the area and how it helped make California a state. Complete the activities on these pages as you read the unit.

What I know about . . .

the California Gold Rush:

Who shaped California in the early 1800s?

Choose three people from the list below. Write one person's name in each box. Then write one fact about the effect that each person had on California history.

John Sutter	Jedediah Smith	James Beckwourth	John Bidwell
John C. Fremont	Pio Pico	Biddy Mason	Helen Hunt Jackson
Mary Tape	Bernarda Ruiz	Sam Brannan	James Marshall
Bennett Riley	Peter Burnett	Louise Clapp	Mariano Guadalupe Vallejo

Complete these sections as you read the unit.

Which person from this unit would you like to interview? Write his or her name below.

Write a question you would like to ask this person.

Now write down two facts about this person.

1.

2.

List three ways the Gold Rush changed California.

1.

2.

3.

In the boxes below, record a major step in California's move toward statehood for each year shown. Notice that 1846 had two major events.

1846	1849	1850
1.		
2.		

I have learned . . .

Name:

H-SS 4.3.1 Identify the locations of Mexican settlements in California and those of other settlements, including Fort Ross and Sutter's Fort.

Lesson 1

Where were California's settlements?

SET THE SCENE How do you think the large cities in California came to be? The Spanish settled areas along the coast. Then Mexico took control and established more settlements. Soon people began to come here from other countries. How did all of these settlers impact California?

Preview the Lesson

Vocabulary

pioneer *(n.)* a person who is one of the first settlers of a part of a country

Vocabulary Activity Write a definition of *pioneer* below in your own words.

People

Ivan Kuskov John Sutter

Reading: Cause and Effect

Cause-and-effect relationships show the connections between events. A *cause* is what makes something happen. An *effect* is what happens as a result of the cause. As you read the lesson, circle words or phrases such as *because, so,* or *as a result* that signal cause-and-effect relationships.

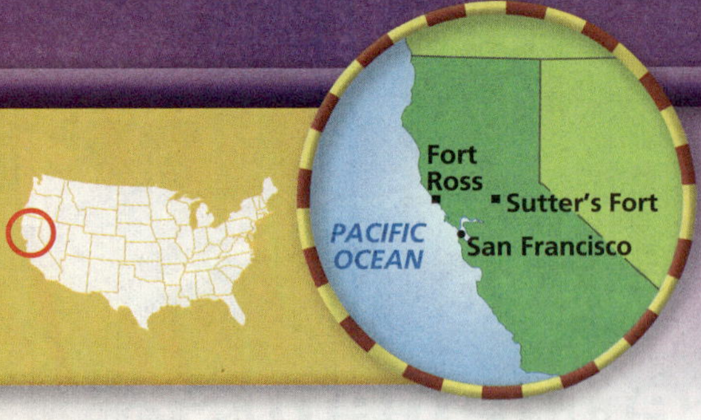

1815 | 1820

1812

1821 Mexico wins independence from Spain.

Russian Settlements

As the Spanish came from present-day Mexico and settled in California from the south, Russian settlers arrived by sea from the northwest. In 1812 Ivan Kuskov (KOOSH kov) led a group of Russian and native Alaskan fur trappers to a place north of San Francisco. The trappers came to the area to hunt sea otters. They built Fort Ross as a trading post. Within ten years, the trappers had caught most of the area's sea otters. They tried to farm the land, but they were unsuccessful. So by the early 1840s they had left the area.

1. How was Fort Ross different from the missions and other settlements in what is now California? *Compare and Contrast*

Today, tourists visit Fort Ross to learn about the early history of California.

1825 1830 1835 1840

1841 Sutter's Fort is built.

Sutter's Fort was the first place many settlers came after they crossed the mountains from the East.

Mexican Settlements

As you have learned, Mexico took over the Spanish missions when it won its independence from Spain in 1821. After that, many Mexicans began to move north to California because they wanted farmland. As a result, many missions became Mexican settlements. These settlements were good places to live, farm, and trade because of their locations near the coast. Over time, cities such as San Diego, Santa Barbara, and San Francisco grew from these settlements.

Sutter's Fort

At about the same time the Russians were leaving California, new pioneers were arriving. A **pioneer** is one of the first settlers of a part of a country. One pioneer was John Sutter. In 1841 he had a fort built that became known as Sutter's Fort. It was located where the Sacramento and American Rivers meet. He sold supplies to people passing through the area.

2. Cause and Effect **Why were the Mexican settlements good places to farm and trade?**

3. Underline details about Sutter's Fort.
Main Idea and Details

Summary

As more people came to California, settlements grew throughout the area. What are some reasons why different groups of settlers came to California in the early 1800s?

Skill

Time Lines

Learn More A time line shows important events that happened over a period of time. Some time lines are horizontal. That means they run from left to right. Others are vertical. A vertical time line lists events along a line that runs up and down. This makes it easy to see the order of events and their relationships to each other.

Try It

Use the time line to answer the following questions:

1. **In the late 1700s, Spain established missions along the California coast. On the time line, circle the year that the first mission was built.** *Sequence*

2. **Underline the city that is located where settlers established a mission in 1776.** *Identify*

3. **Draw a box around the name of the activity that brought the Russians to the area in 1812.** *Identify*

4. **How many years passed between the time the first group of American settlers arrived in California and the time California became a territory of the United States?** *Sequence*

____

1750

1769 Junípero Serra establishes the first mission in what is now California.

1776 Settlers build a mission and fort in what is now San Francisco.

1796 The *Otter* is the first American ship to reach the coast of the California territory.

1800

1812 Russians build a fur-trading post at Fort Ross in an area north of San Francisco.

1821 California becomes part of Mexico.

1841 The first organized group of American settlers arrives in California.

1848 The United States gains the California territory from Mexico.

1850

Name:

H-SS 4.3.2 Compare how and why people traveled to California and the routes they traveled (e.g., James Beckwourth, John Bidwell, John C. Fremont, Pio Pico).

How and why did people travel to California?

SET THE SCENE What would it be like to travel from the East Coast to the West Coast without trains, cars, or planes? As more settlements were built in California, more people wanted to come to the area. What led settlers to cross deserts, mountains, and oceans to get here?

Preview the Lesson

Vocabulary

expand *(v.)* to grow larger

migrate *(v.)* to move from one place to another

immigrate *(v.)* to come into another country to live

Vocabulary Activity Synonyms are words that have the same or almost the same meanings. Circle a synonym above for the word *increase*.

People

Pio Pico
Jedediah Smith
John Bidwell
James Beckwourth
John C. Fremont

Reading: Compare and Contrast

When you *compare* two or more things, you tell how they are alike. When you *contrast* two or more things, you tell how they are different. As you read page 72, underline the sentences that contrast the different reasons why people came to California.

1770 1780 1790

1775

The United States Grows

In the early 1800s the United States started to **expand,** or grow larger. Many settlers began migrating west. To **migrate** means to move from one place to another. Some of these settlers immigrated to the United States from other countries. To **immigrate** means to come into another country to live. Some American settlers immigrated to Mexican California to find land they could farm. Others planned to sell supplies to other settlers. Some people just wanted to explore the western regions. Many wanted to try something new and different.

During this time, there was no easy way to get to California from the East Coast of the United States. Most ships had to sail around Cape Horn at the tip of South America. That trip was about 17,000 miles and took up to eight months to complete. A shortcut could be taken by crossing the Isthmus (IS mus) of Panama, a narrow strip of land between the Pacific and Atlantic Oceans.

1. What did many of the people who migrated west in the early 1800s have in common?

Compare and Contrast

This historical map shows the Isthmus of Panama.

1800 1810 1820 1830 1840

1841 John Bidwell leaves Independence, Missouri, for California.

Trails Leading West

Most American pioneers took a more direct land route west to California. A horse-drawn wagon could get here from the state of Missouri in three to six months. Along the way, land travelers had to cross rivers, mountains, and deserts. Mexican settlers came to California from the south. The family of Pio Pico was part of Juan Bautista de Anza's group of Mexican pioneers that came here in 1775. Later, Pico became the last Mexican governor, or top leader, of California.

People wanted to find new routes to California. In 1826 Jedediah Smith led the first group of American trappers who came overland to California through the Utah and Mojave Deserts. In 1841 John Bidwell was in the first wagon train of settlers to come here from Independence, Missouri. John C. Fremont traveled all over the area making maps for the U.S. government in the early 1840s. Fremont wrote reports that made Americans in the East interested in coming to the West. James Beckwourth was an African American scout, or guide, who led settlers west during the 1850s.

In the 1850s, James Beckwourth led settlers through a mountain pass in the Sierra Nevada that was later named for him.

2. Describe what you think it would be like to travel to California by horse or horse-drawn wagon.

Draw Conclusions

Summary

As new trails were created, more Americans became interested in moving west. Why do you think a pioneer or early settler would risk the dangers and challenges of going to California in the mid-1800s?

Skill

Routes on Maps

Learn More Many people who came west started their trips in Independence, Missouri. What routes do you think people took to California?

When you study routes on maps, use the map legend to figure out the different routes. Understanding the map legend will help you tell one route from another.

Try It

Suppose you were a settler heading west. Use the map to answer the following questions:

1. **Trace the route you would take from Independence to Sacramento.** *Interpret*
2. **Which of the trails is farthest north?** *Identify*

   ____

3. **Circle the California city at the end of the Old Spanish Trail.** *Identify*

Markers, such as this one in Colorado, can still be seen along what used to be the Santa Fe Trail.

Name:

Lesson
3

H-SS 4.3.3 Analyze the effects of the Gold Rush on settlements, daily life, politics, and the physical environment (e.g., using biographies of John Sutter, Mariano Guadalupe Vallejo, Louise Clapp).

How did the discovery of gold affect California?

SET THE SCENE What event do you think changed the history of California forever? One day in 1848, a man found a few small pieces of gold in a river near present-day Sacramento. Soon many Americans were rushing west. Would you have joined them in their search for gold?

Preview the Lesson

Vocabulary

entrepreneur *(n.)* a person who starts a new business with the hope of making money

boomtown *(n.)* a town that grows rapidly as a result of new business

Vocabulary Activity *Boom* means "sudden rapid growth." How does knowing the meaning of the word *boom* help you understand *boomtown*? Explain your answer.

People

James Marshall
Sam Brannan
Levi Strauss
Mariano Guadalupe Vallejo

Reading: Cause and Effect

Sometimes a cause can have more than one effect. An effect can also have more than one cause. Look for cause-and-effect relationships as you read the lesson. Circle sentences that describe different effects of the California Gold Rush.

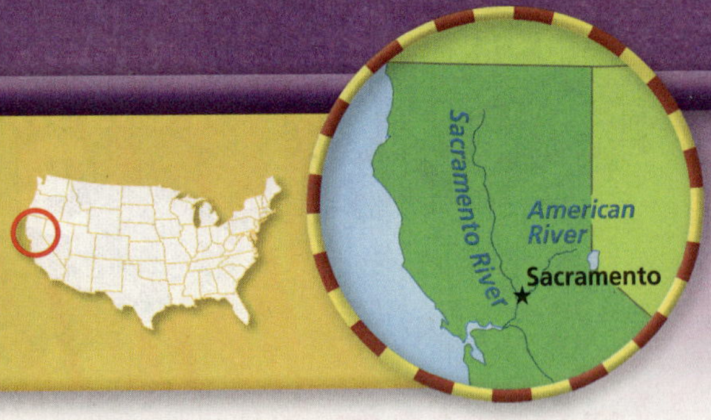

The Discovery of Gold

The story of gold in California started with a very small discovery. In January 1848, James Marshall was building a new sawmill for John Sutter. The mill was located in Coloma, next to the American River. It would provide lumber for Sutter's Fort in present-day Sacramento, about fifty miles away. One day, Marshall found some shiny rocks the size of peas in the river. He had them tested. The rocks had gold in them.

1. Cause and Effect **What part did John Sutter have in the discovery of gold in California?**

"Gold Fever" Spreads

People reacted differently to Marshall's discovery. Sutter wanted to keep the gold a secret because he did not want people rushing to the area. However, Sam Brannan had a different plan. Brannan was an **entrepreneur,** or a person who starts a new business with the hope of making money. When Brannan heard about the gold, he bought a lot of mining tools to sell. In order to create excitement and sell his tools, he ran through the streets of San Francisco yelling and carrying a bottle of gold dust. Many people thought they could find their own gold too. Brannan made sure they bought their gold-mining tools from him.

2. Cause and Effect **Why did Sam Brannan run through the streets of San Francisco with a bottle of gold dust?**

Gold was found in 1848 near the site of Sutter's Mill.

1847 | 1848 | 1849

1848

1849 The California Gold Rush begins.

As more people came to California in search of gold, cities such as San Francisco grew quickly.

California's Population "Booms"

In a short time, a rush of newcomers came to California in what became known as the California Gold Rush of 1849. These new settlers were called "forty-niners."

Soon after, the cities of San Francisco, Stockton, and Sacramento grew quickly and became boomtowns. A **boomtown** is a town that grows rapidly as a result of new business. Their growth came about because of the gold business and the many settlers who came to the area.

Many more men than women came here during the Gold Rush. One woman who came west with her husband was Louise Clapp. Clapp wrote letters to her sister using the name "Dame Shirley." The letters described life in the mining towns and camps during the Gold Rush. Clapp's letters were later published in a San Francisco magazine.

3. Cause and Effect **What effect did the Gold Rush have on cities in California?**

Life as a Forty-Niner

Life as a miner was hard. Miners had land claims that gave them the right to mine an area of land. But digging or panning for gold was slow, boring, and often dangerous work. While panning, a miner stood bent over in a cold stream all day long. After all that, the miner might have only a little bit of gold dust at the end of the day. Miners also had to watch out for fool's gold, or iron pyrite, which looks like gold but is worthless.

Much of the gold mined in California was found in what was called the mother lode. A lode is a supply or deposit. The mother lode was a strip of rich gold deposits in the Sierra Nevada.

4. How would you describe the life of a miner? Explain your answer. *Main Idea and Details*

Miners often lived in tents in mining camps.

Fool's gold fooled many miners into thinking they had found gold.

California's Mother Lode

Locate and circle the mother lode on the map .

Rich and Poor

Few miners got rich during the Gold Rush. Most of the people who made a lot of money were shop owners and entrepreneurs. They sold tools and supplies to miners.

One entrepreneur was Levi Strauss. He saw that miners needed tough work pants for mining gold. Strauss had riveted denim pants made and began to sell them. They became popular for miners. Strauss's company still exists in San Francisco today.

John Sutter, on the other hand, did not get rich from the Gold Rush. He wanted to build a farming business around Sutter's Fort. But in the 1850s, few people came to California to farm. Most of them just wanted to find gold. Sutter's Fort was abandoned as people moved out into the surrounding area to look for gold.

Changes in Government

The Gold Rush also changed how California was governed. Mariano Guadalupe Vallejo (vah YAY ho) was a Mexican born in California. In the 1840s Vallejo became powerful in California and helped govern the area. However, the Gold Rush brought many American settlers to the region in a short time. American settlers soon outnumbered Mexicans such as Vallejo. As more and more Americans moved to California, their power and influence in government increased.

5. In what ways did people other than the miners benefit from the Gold Rush?

Main Idea and Details

Levi Strauss added metal rivets to denim pants to make them stronger.

6. Cause and Effect **How did the Gold Rush affect government in California?**

Summary

The Gold Rush changed California in many ways in a very short period of time. Describe what you think the positive and negative effects were of the Gold Rush on California.

Primary Source

Memoirs: Luzena Stanley Wilson

Learn More Memoirs are written by a person about events in his or her lifetime. Luzena Stanley Wilson started the El Dorado Hotel in the mining town of Nevada City in the spring of 1850. She told her daughter about this experience years later. In the passage below, Wilson explains how she started her business.

This is the only known photograph of Luzena Stanley Wilson.

Use the journal entry to answer the following questions:

1. What do you think made Wilson want to set up a rival hotel? *Interpret*

____

____

____

____

2. How do you think Wilson's business affected the town of Nevada City? *Analyze*

____

____

____

____

"I determined to set up a rival [competing] hotel. So I bought two boards from a precious pile belonging to a man who was building the second wooden house in town. With my own hands I chopped stakes, drove them into the ground, and set up my table. I bought provisions [food] at a neighboring store, and when my husband came back at night he found . . . twenty miners eating at my table. Each man as he rose put a dollar in my hand and said I might count him as a permanent customer. I called my hotel 'El Dorado.'"

—From *Luzena Stanley Wilson, '49er, 1937*

Name:

H-SS 4.3.4 Study the lives of women who helped build early California (e.g., Biddy Mason).

Lesson 4

How did women help California grow?

SET THE SCENE What would it be like to travel somewhere far away? At first, only a few women traveled to California. However, some of those women had a lasting impact. What was life like for women in California in the mid-1800s?

Preview the Lesson

Vocabulary

slavery *(n.)* the practice of owning people and forcing them to work without pay

compromise *(n.)* a solution to a disagreement in which each side gives up a part of what it wants

fugitive *(n.)* a person who tries to escape from an authority

petition *(v.)* to officially ask someone to do something

Vocabulary Activity Use one of the vocabulary words above to complete the following sentence:

When the two students disagreed about who should play with the ball,

they made a ________________ *and agreed to take turns.*

People

Helen Hunt Jackson
Biddy Mason
Mary Tape

Reading: Fact and Opinion

Writers often use facts and opinions in their writing. A *fact* is a statement that is known to be true. An *opinion* is a person's belief or judgment. As you read the first paragraph on page 82, underline the facts in the text.

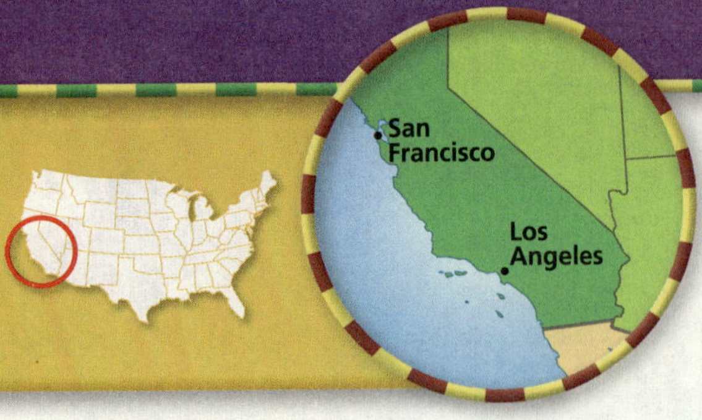

Traveling West

Women who traveled to California in the 1800s faced many of the same challenges as men. These included illnesses and harsh weather. In a newly-settled area, building new homes, farms, and businesses was difficult work.

Many women came west because their husbands wanted to mine for gold, but some traveled here on their own. Women who came to California might have found a job cooking or doing laundry. Others ran boarding houses, where travelers and settlers could spend the night. A few women also mined for gold.

Making a Difference

Some women worked to solve large problems in California. Bernarda Ruiz lived in Santa Barbara during a time when Mexico was at war with the United States. Ruiz wanted to see an end to this war. So in 1847, she helped arrange a peace meeting between leaders from both sides.

Helen Hunt Jackson was a writer who thought the treatment of American Indians was unfair. In 1884 she wrote a popular novel, called *Ramona,* about the harsh lives of California Indians. Jackson's book is still celebrated in our state today at an annual festival in Hemet.

Helen Hunt Jackson traveled around the state to learn about the treatment of California Indians.

1. Based on the text, write an opinion statement about women who traveled west.

Fact and Opinion

2. List similarities and differences between Bernarda Ruiz and Helen Hunt Jackson.

Compare and Contrast

Mary Tape was a Chinese immigrant who lived in San Francisco in the late 1800s. She was upset that her Chinese American daughter was not allowed to attend public school. Tape and her husband argued that the city should change this rule. Because of Tape's efforts, a school was created for Chinese and other Asian students.

Mary Tape and her husband, seen here with their family, worked for the fair treatment of Asian Americans.

Gaining Freedom

Bridget "Biddy" Mason was another woman who made a difference. Mason was born into slavery in about 1818. **Slavery** is the practice of owning people and forcing them to work without pay. In 1851 Mason's owner took her to California, where slavery was not allowed. A year earlier, when California had become a state, people disagreed about whether or not slavery should be allowed. At that time the United States was made up of fifteen states that allowed slavery and fifteen states that did not. California's decision about slavery would end the balance.

The Compromise of 1850 solved this problem. A **compromise** is a solution to a disagreement in which each side gives up a part of what it wants. The Compromise of 1850 said that California would be a free state, which would not allow slavery. However, it also said that free states would have to obey fugitive slave laws. A **fugitive** is a person who tries to escape from an authority. The laws said that enslaved people who were fugitives must be captured and returned to their owners.

Because Biddy Mason lived in California, a free state, she was able to petition for her freedom. To **petition** means to officially ask someone to do something. Mason won her freedom and became a successful landowner in Los Angeles.

3. How did Biddy Mason become a free woman?

Main Idea and Details

Summary

Women also came to California during the Gold Rush, and some made a difference in our state's history. How did women contribute to California's development in the 1800s?

Biography

Bridget "Biddy" Mason, 1818–1891

Learn More After Biddy Mason gained her freedom, she moved to Los Angeles. Mason worked hard as a nurse and saved her money until she could afford to buy land. She became one of the first African American women in Los Angeles to own property.

With the money she earned, Mason founded the first African American church in Los Angeles. She also donated to charities, visited prisoners, and helped to feed the poor. Many people called her "Auntie Mason" or "Grandma Mason" due to her giving spirit.

Use the information about Biddy Mason to answer the following questions:

1. **Circle the achievements of Biddy Mason that make her a good role model for people today.** *Identify*
2. **How do you think Biddy Mason's life was different from those of many other African American women in the 1800s?** *Analyze*

____

____

____

____

____

____

Name:

H-SS 4.3.5 Discuss how California became a state and how its new government differed from those during the Spanish and Mexican periods.

Lesson 5

How did California's government change?

SET THE SCENE Today as a Californian, you live in the United States, not Mexico. Do you know how California became a state?

Preview the Lesson

Vocabulary

republic *(n.)* a type of government in which citizens elect leaders to represent them

constitution *(n.)* a written plan for governing a country or state

delegate *(n.)* a person who is chosen to speak for others

ratify *(v.)* to officially approve

representative *(n.)* someone who is chosen to act for someone else

Vocabulary Activity An *antonym* is a word that means the opposite of another word. Circle an antonym above for the word *reject.*

People

Bennett Riley

Peter H. Burnett

Reading: Cause and Effect

As you read, ask yourself questions to help you understand what makes things happen. When studying an event, ask: "What caused this event to happen? What happened as a result?" As you read the lesson, underline sentences that tell the effects of a rush of Americans to California.

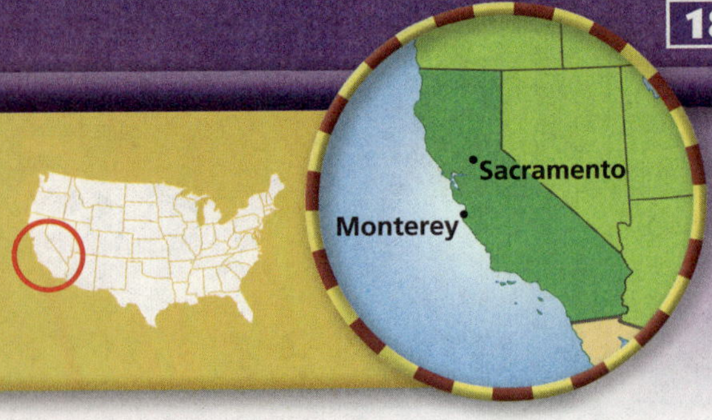

1846

1847

1846 The Bear Flag Revolt begins. The Mexican-American War begins.

Changes in Control of California

Big changes were happening in California before the Gold Rush. In the early 1840s this land was part of Mexico. However, some American settlers living here wanted California to be an independent republic. A **republic** is a type of government in which citizens elect leaders to represent them. So in 1846, a small group of Americans started a revolt, or uprising, against Mexico. This was called the Bear Flag Revolt.

In 1846 Mexico and the United States fought a war over their border. The United States won the Mexican-American War, and in 1848, Mexico signed the Treaty of Guadalupe Hidalgo. Mexico's territories from New Mexico to California became part of the United States.

1. Cause and Effect **What effect did the end of the Mexican-American War have on California?**

The Treaty of Guadalupe Hidalgo, 1848

Trace the outline of where the state of California is today.

1848 1849 1850

1848 The Mexican-American War ends.

1849 Delegates from California write a state constitution.

1850

Statehood

After California became part of the United States, Bennett Riley was appointed the military governor of the territory. In 1849 Riley called a meeting to create a state constitution. A **constitution** is a written plan for governing or running a state or country. Forty-eight delegates met in Monterey to write a constitution for California. A **delegate** is a person who is chosen to speak for others. On September 9, 1850, the U.S. government decided to **ratify,** or officially approve, the California Constitution. California became the thirty-first state of the United States.

When California became a state, its people elected Peter H. Burnett as their first governor. They sent representatives to the U.S. Congress in Washington, D.C. A **representative** is someone who is chosen to act for someone else. Sacramento became the state capital in 1854.

2. Why do you think California needed to write a constitution before it could become a state? *Draw Conclusions*

After becoming a state, California moved its capital several times to places such as Benicia, shown below, before finally moving to Sacramento.

Summary

Many things changed in California in the 1840s. Describe the events leading up to California's becoming a state, starting with the Bear Flag Revolt.

Citizenship

California Under Three Governments

Learn More When you live somewhere, you live under the rules and government of the country that controls that area. Over the past 450 years, California has been a part of Spain, Mexico, and the United States. Each country governed the area differently. For example, when Spain controlled California, Spain was a monarchy. That meant that Spain and all its lands were run by a king or queen from a family of rulers. The king or queen would then appoint, or choose, a governor to run smaller areas of land, such as California.

Use the chart to answer the following questions:

1. **Circle the words that tell how Spain gained control of California.** *Summarize*

2. **What type of government has controlled California longer, a monarchy or a republic?** *Apply*

____

Governments of California

Country	Years of Control	How Control Was Gained	Type of Government	Head of Government
Spain	1542–1821	Spanish explorers claimed the area that would become California.	Monarchy	King or Queen of Spain
Mexico	1821–1848	Mexico won independence from Spain and took control of California.	1821–1823: Monarchy 1824–1848: Republic	President of Mexico
United States	1848–Present	The United States won the Mexican-American War and took control of California.	Republic	State Level: governor National Level: President

Name:

Study Journal

Unit 4

In this unit you will learn how California's industries grew. You will also see how California's economy, government, and culture have developed since 1850. Record information on these pages as you read the unit.

What I know about . . .

California's development:

How has technology changed?

Communication	Transportation
Past	Past
Present	Present

Industry	Services
Past	Past
Present	Present

Complete these sections as you read the unit.

Draw a picture and write about the most interesting person in the unit.

Circle one item below and write two facts abouts its development.

- Schools
- Culture
- Government
- Aqueducts
- Farming
- Immigration

1.

2.

Write the events in order in the time line boxes below.

1850 | 1875 | 1900 | 1925

1850
California opens the state's first public school in San Francisco.

1869

1929

I have learned . . .

Name:

H-SS 4.4.1 Understand the story and lasting influence of the Pony Express, Overland Mail Service, Western Union, and the building of the transcontinental railroad, including the contributions of Chinese workers to its construction.

Lesson 1

How did the movement of people and ideas change in California?

SET THE SCENE Can you picture life without a television, a radio, or the Internet? In the 1800s, none of these things were around. Californians did not even have a regular mail service. How did people learn about news or stay in touch with each other?

Preview the Lesson

Vocabulary

communication *(n.)* the way that people send and receive information

technology *(n.)* the use of scientific knowledge to solve problems

telegraph *(n.)* a machine that sends signals along wires using electricity

engineer *(n.)* a person who designs structures such as roads, bridges, and machines

investor *(n.)* a person who gives money to a company with the hope of making money later

Vocabulary Activity The root word *graph* in *telegraph* comes from the Greek word that means "write." Think of other words with the root *graph*.

People

John Butterfield
Samuel Morse
Theodore Judah
Leland Stanford
Charles Crocker
Collis Huntington
Mark Hopkins

Reading: Sequence

Writers present information in a *sequence,* or certain order. Sometimes they use dates and time-order words such as *first, then,* and *after* to show the sequence of events. As you read, circle dates that help you keep track of the important events in California.

1858

1859

1858 The Butterfield Overland Stage Company reaches California.

Distant California

When California became a state in 1850, few settlers lived between here and the Mississippi River. The distance between our state and the rest of the country made travel to California difficult. Communication was also hard. **Communication** is the way that people send and receive information. Contact improved during the 1850s and 1860s due to **technology,** which is the use of scientific knowledge to solve problems. Communication between California and other states became faster.

Communication with California

The first regular overland mail service to California was called the Butterfield Overland Stage Company. John Butterfield started it in 1858. The service carried mail and passengers in stagecoaches, or closed carriages, pulled by horses. It took mail about twenty-four days to travel the 2,800 miles between towns near the Mississippi River and San Francisco.

Another important mail service was the Pony Express. Starting in April 1860, riders on horseback carried mail between St. Joseph, Missouri, and Sacramento. First, a rider carried the mail about twelve miles. Then he changed horses and rode another twelve miles. After one rider had gone about seventy-five miles, another rider took over. The mail traveled an average of 200 miles a day and took nine to ten days to get to California.

1. When did travel to California and communication with its people improve?

Main Ideas and Details

2. Sequence **Underline the sequence of events for a Pony Express rider.**

Many different overland services carried mail to the West during the late 1800s.

1860 | 1861 | 1862 | 1863

1860

____

____

1861 Telegraph service reaches California and puts an end to the Pony Express.

This letter was sent from San Francisco to New York City in 1861 using the Pony Express.

Use the map scale to calculate the distance of the Pony Express route.

Communication Improves

A new technology called the telegraph replaced the Pony Express, which lasted only eighteen months. A **telegraph** is a machine that sends signals along wires using electricity. Samuel Morse developed a practical telegraph in the 1830s. It was not used in California until the 1860s. The Western Union Telegraph Company built the first transcontinental telegraph line. Something that is *transcontinental* crosses a continent, such as North America. The line started carrying messages between San Francisco and the East Coast in October 1861.

3. Why do you think the telegraph replaced the Pony Express? *Draw Conclusions*

____

____

____

____

Samuel Morse used a telegraph sounder like this one to send signals.

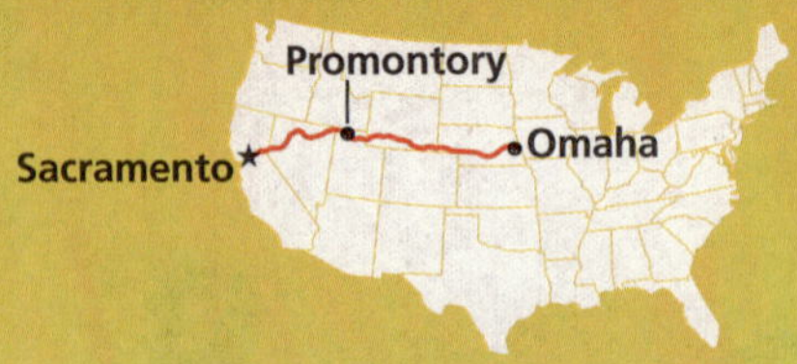

1865 The building of the transcontinental railroad begins from Omaha.

The Transcontinental Railroad

The telegraph made communication with California faster and easier, but traveling here still took a long time. That would soon change thanks to a young engineer named Theodore Judah. An **engineer** is a person who designs structures such as roads, bridges, and machines. Judah was building railroad lines around Sacramento in the 1850s, but he had a bigger dream. He thought that the United States should have a transcontinental railroad system—or one that stretched across the country. There was already railroad service throughout the East, but there was no railroad from the middle of the country to the West Coast.

Starting the Railroad

To build his railroad, Judah needed **investors,** or people who give money to a company with the hope of making money later. He found four men to invest in his plan. Leland Stanford, Charles Crocker, Collis Huntington, and Mark Hopkins became known as the Big Four. They formed the Central Pacific Railroad Company. Work on the railroad started on January 8, 1863. Workers laid track eastward from Sacramento. In 1865 the Union Pacific Railroad Company began to lay track westward from Omaha, Nebraska.

4. Why do you think people called Theodore Judah's railroad the "transcontinental" railroad? *Draw Conclusions*

5. How did the Big Four impact transportation in the United States? *Draw Conclusions*

1869 The transcontinental railroad is completed.

Thousands of workers came to California to work on the transcontinental railroad.

Railroad Workers

Many laborers were needed to build the transcontinental railroad. At first, the Central Pacific Railroad Company did not have enough workers. So in 1865, the company began hiring immigrants from China who were willing to come to California to work.

About 10,000 Chinese workers came to California to help build the Central Pacific Railroad. They built tracks across the Sierra Nevada. They did this by digging tunnels and using explosives to blast through mountainsides. The Chinese worked long hours underground. It was dangerous work, and many of them died. Meanwhile, other workers, including many Irish immigrants, were laying Union Pacific tracks west across the Great Plains.

Finally, on May 10, 1869, the two tracks met in Promontory, Utah. A golden railroad spike connected the last piece of track. At last, the railroad line was finished. Unfortunately, Theodore Judah died in 1863, and he never saw the completion of his dream.

6. Underline details in the text that describe why railroad work was dangerous in the Sierra Nevada.

Main Idea and Details

Summary

New technologies allowed news, people, and goods to travel more easily between California and the rest of the country. Describe how transportation and communication technologies strengthened California's link with the rest of the country.

Primary Source

Artifacts: Train Schedule

Learn More You have already learned that documents and photographs can be primary sources. They were written or taken at the time an event happened. Schedules are artifacts, which can also be primary sources. Have you ever looked at a train schedule, or timetable, so that you know when the next train arrives or departs?

In the 1800s, people also used train schedules. The schedule below lists the arrivals and departures for the Central Pacific Railroad between Sacramento and Newcastle. This route was one of the first sections of the transcontinental railroad that was put into operation. Use the train schedule to answer the questions below.

CENTRAL PACIFIC RAILROAD.

No. 1, TIME CARD No. 1.

To take effect Monday June 6th, 1864, at 5 A. M.

TRAINS EASTWARD.					TRAINS WESTWARD.		
Frt and Pass No 3	Frt and Pass No 2	Pass & Mail No 1.		STATIONS.	Frt and Pass No 1	Pass & Mail No 2.	Frt and Pass No 3.
5 P M leave	1 P M leave	6.15 A M, L	......	Sacramento.	...... 8.45 A M arr	12 M arr.	6.40 P M ar.
5.50 5.55 } mt frt	2.15	3.55	18	Junction.	18 3	11.20	5.55 5.50 } mt. Ft
6.09	2.38	7.05	22	Rocklin.	4 7.40	11.07	5.37
6.22	2.55	7.15 meet F	25	Pino.	3 7.15 mt pass	10.56	5.25
6.40	3.30 P M arr	7.30 A M arr	31	Newcastle.	6 3.45 A M, L	10.30 A M, L	5 P M, L

Trains No. 2 and 3 east, and 1 and 3 west, daily, except Sunday.
Trains No. 1 east and 2 west, daily.

LELAND STANFORD, President.

1. **On the timetable, circle the date service began. Draw a star next to the name of one of the Big Four.** *Identify*
2. **If you left on Train No. 1 from Sacramento going east, what time would you arrive in Rocklin station?** *Interpret*

____

Name:

H-SS 4.4.2 Explain how the Gold Rush transformed the economy of California, including the types of products produced and consumed, changes in towns (e.g., Sacramento, San Francisco), and economic conflicts between diverse groups of people.

How did the Gold Rush change California's economy?

SET THE SCENE It was an ordinary day in 1848 when James Marshall spotted gold in the American River. Later, he wrote, "My eye was caught by something shining in the bottom of the ditch. . . . It made my heart thump, for I was certain it was gold." How did the discovery of gold change California?

Preview the Lesson

Vocabulary

import *(v.)* to bring something in from another country or area to sell

product *(n.)* something that is made, grown, or taken from nature and sold

merchant *(n.)* a person who buys and sells goods

diversity *(n.)* many different types of people or things

discrimination *(n.)* treating someone differently from someone else in an unfair way

export *(v.)* to send something to another country or area to be sold

Vocabulary Activity The root word *port* means "carry." How does this help you understand the definition of *import* from the list above?

Reading: Fact and Opinion

A *fact* is something that is generally believed to be true. An *opinion* is a person's belief or judgment. It is important to know the difference between facts and opinions so that you can understand an author's purpose in writing. Look at the advertisements above. Circle words that signal opinions.

California's Changing Economy

California's economy grew quickly during the Gold Rush. Before 1848 there were few businesses. People imported many of the goods they needed. To **import** means to bring something in from another country or area to sell. But during the Gold Rush, miners needed products such as tools, tents, and sturdy clothes. A **product** is something that is made, grown, or taken from nature and sold. These mining products were provided to the growing population by merchants. A **merchant** is a person who buys and sells goods. To meet these needs, people in California began making some of their own products. People also opened many new hotels, laundries, restaurants, and banks.

1. Use facts from the text to support the following statement: "The Gold Rush changed California's economy." *Fact and Opinion*

In 1849 San Francisco was a town with few homes and businesses.

Growth of Towns and Cities

As you have learned, the Gold Rush of 1849 caused the population of California cities to boom. Between 1848 and 1849, San Francisco's population rose from 800 to 25,000.

Sacramento became a trade center for farm products and later a center for transportation and communication. Between 1870 and 1900, its population grew from 16,000 to 29,000.

The population of Los Angeles grew as well. About 1,600 people lived there in 1850, and the city grew slowly over the next twenty years. In the 1870s and 1880s, train service reached Southern California. That made it easier to travel between Southern California and the rest of the country. People started coming from the East and Midwest to Los Angeles. By 1900, more than 100,000 people lived in Los Angeles.

By the 1870s, San Francisco was a busy city.

2. Sequence **Complete the chart to show the population growth of Sacramento and Los Angeles in the late 1800s. Circle the city that had the greater growth.**

SACRAMENTO		LOS ANGELES
	1850	Population
	1860	
Population	1870	
	1880	
	1890	
Population	1900	Population

Different Groups in California

In the 1800s, California's population began to show a lot of diversity. **Diversity** means many different types of people or things. People from countries such as Mexico, China, Ireland, Germany, Italy, and Russia all came to live and work here. Life was hard for many of these groups. Pay was low, and there was much discrimination. **Discrimination** means treating someone differently from someone else in an unfair way. The discrimination in California was mostly directed at Chinese and Mexican immigrants.

During the mid- to late 1800s, many Japanese farmers came to California to find jobs. They were good farmers and had much success. Other farmers felt that the success of the Japanese farms hurt their businesses. So in 1913, the state passed a law that kept Japanese immigrants from buying land.

3. What problems made life hard for groups of people who came here from other countries? *Main Idea and Details*

Japanese farmers grew crops such as strawberries, as shown in this photograph.

By the late 1800s, California's farming economy was booming.

The Farming Boom

Farming in California also changed after the Gold Rush. Why? Because the state's population grew during the Gold Rush, and more food needed to be produced. Also, when the Gold Rush ended, miners began to look for other work, and many of them became farmers. By 1860 the number of farms had grown to nearly 19,000.

Because California has a warm and sunny climate and good soil, a variety of crops can be grown here. In the early 1860s, farmers began to grow wheat, which was the top farm product until the 1890s. The citrus business, which included oranges and lemons, started in the 1870s. By that time, the transcontinental railroad allowed California farmers to export their crops to the Midwest and East. To **export** means to send something to another country or area to be sold. Exporting helped expand the farmers' businesses. By 1900 California was a leading producer of apples, apricots, cherries, peaches, pears, and plums.

4. Circle details in the text that describe why farming changed after the Gold Rush.
Main Idea and Details

Growing and selling fruit became a big business in California, as shown in these advertisements from about 1900.

Summary

Although the Gold Rush eventually ended, people in California found other ways to make money. Describe how the Gold Rush changed California's economy.

Skill

Line Graphs

Learn More A line graph presents information visually. It is a useful way to show changes in information over time. Graphs also can help governments keep track of certain facts, such as growth in population over time.

The line graph below shows how the population of San Francisco grew from 1850 to 1900. The years are listed along the bottom of the graph. The population in thousands is listed along the left side of the graph. Each dot shows the population in a certain year. The line connecting the dots shows how the population has changed over the years.

Try It

Use the graph to answer the questions below.

1. **About how many people lived in San Francisco in 1850?** *Identify*

   ____

2. **Underline the year in which San Francisco's population reached 150,000.** *Interpret*
3. **Circle the point on the graph when San Francisco's population doubled from what it was in 1870.** *Analyze*
4. **About how many more people lived in San Francisco in 1900 than in 1860?** *Analyze*

   ____

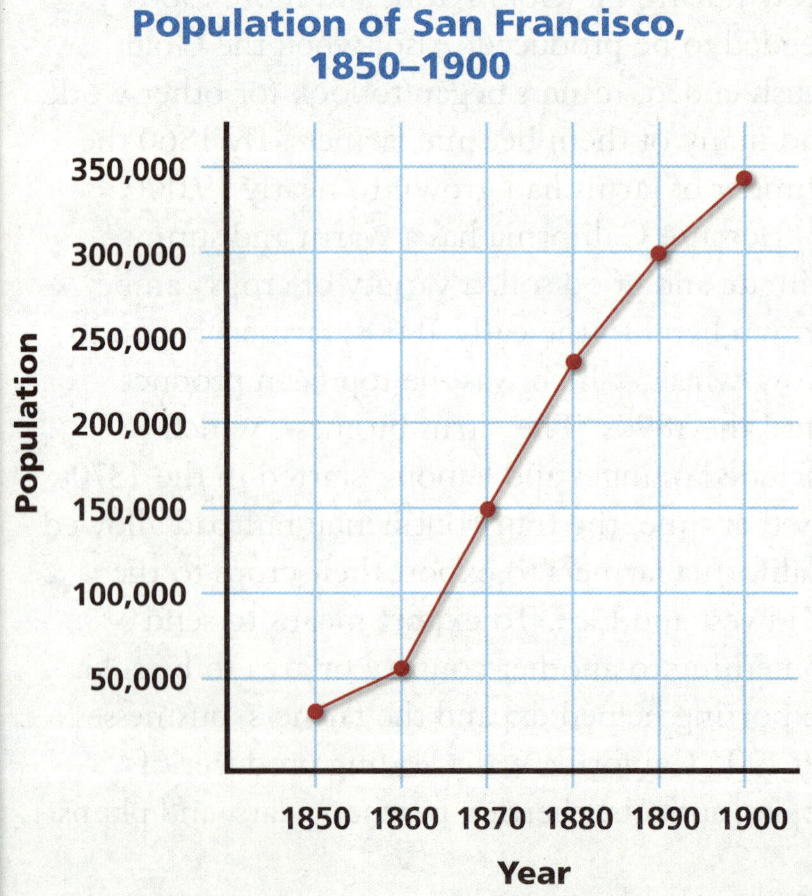

Name:

H-SS 4.4.3 Discuss immigration and migration to California between 1850 and 1900, including the diverse composition of those who came; the countries of origin and their relative locations; and conflicts and accords among the diverse groups (e.g., the 1882 Chinese Exclusion Act).

Lesson 3

How did different people coming to California affect our state?

SET THE SCENE Look around your neighborhood or your classroom. Do you see people from different backgrounds? During and after the Gold Rush, many people from all over the world came to California. How did their diversity help build our state?

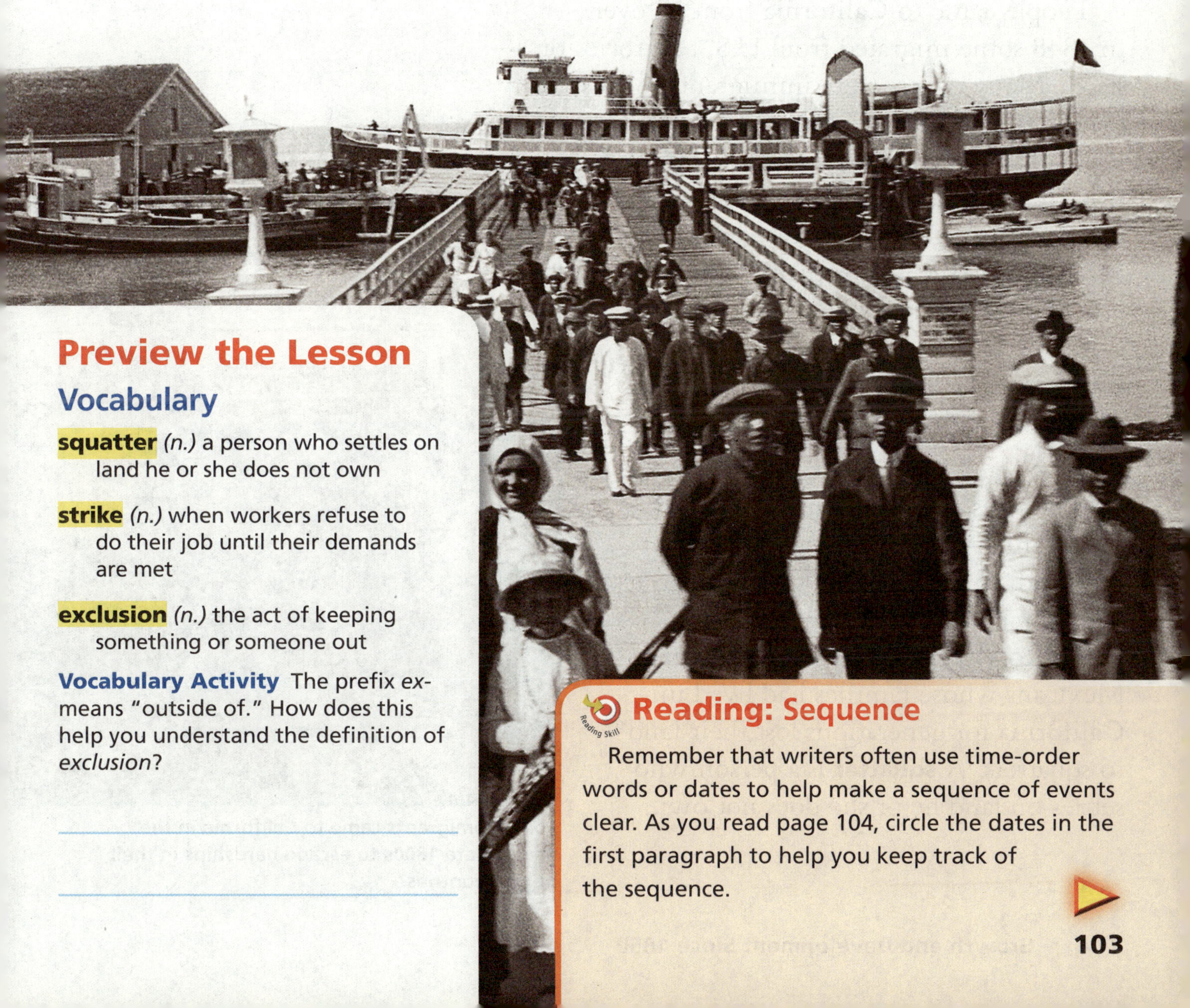

Preview the Lesson

Vocabulary

squatter *(n.)* a person who settles on land he or she does not own

strike *(n.)* when workers refuse to do their job until their demands are met

exclusion *(n.)* the act of keeping something or someone out

Vocabulary Activity The prefix *ex-* means "outside of." How does this help you understand the definition of *exclusion*?

____

____

Reading: Sequence

Reading Skill

Remember that writers often use time-order words or dates to help make a sequence of events clear. As you read page 104, circle the dates in the first paragraph to help you keep track of the sequence.

Immigration from 1850 to 1890s

As you have learned, the Gold Rush caused a huge increase in California's population. In the 1840s, there were about 15,000 people living here in addition to the California Indians. By 1850 about 77,600 more people had arrived. In 1860 the population had reached 380,000.

People came to California from all over. In 1848 some migrated from U.S. territories or states. Many others were immigrants, or people from other countries. South Americans from Peru and Chile lived alongside Europeans from Italy, Ireland, Germany, and Russia. Chinese immigration increased after 1850, and by the 1870s, there were more than 49,000 Chinese living here. At that time, the Chinese and the Irish were California's two largest immigrant groups.

Immigrants Face Challenges

The lives of immigrants were hard. For example, it was not easy for them to buy land. In the late 1800s, many Chinese were forced off their farms and into "Chinatowns" in cities. Likewise, many Mexicans whose families had lived in California for generations lost their land to squatters. A **squatter** is a person who settles on land he or she does not own.

1. Sequence **Use dates to describe the immigration of different groups to California.**

Some immigrants came to California in the mid- to late 1800s to escape hardships in their home countries.

Thousands of Chinese immigrants came to California to find work.

Immigrants often had problems finding jobs. They had to take jobs that did not pay well. Many times they received unfair treatment at work. In 1867 nearly 2,000 Chinese railroad workers went on **strike,** which means they refused to do their jobs until their demands were met. They wanted the same treatment as the other workers, such as equal pay and work hours. But the Chinese railroad strike failed.

Many immigrant workers faced unfair laws. In 1850 the Foreign Miners Tax made immigrants pay twenty dollars a month to work in mines. Many of them could not pay the tax and had to stop mining. In 1882 the Chinese Exclusion Act discriminated against Chinese workers and stopped them from coming to the United States. **Exclusion** is the act of keeping something or someone out. This exclusion law lasted until 1943.

2. How did some Chinese railroad workers stand up for their rights in 1867?
Main Idea and Details

Summary

Between 1850 and 1890, immigrants from all over the world came to California. Many of them faced great hardships and discrimination. Describe what life was like for immigrants in California in the mid- to late 1800s.

Primary Source

Documents: Chinese Exclusion Act

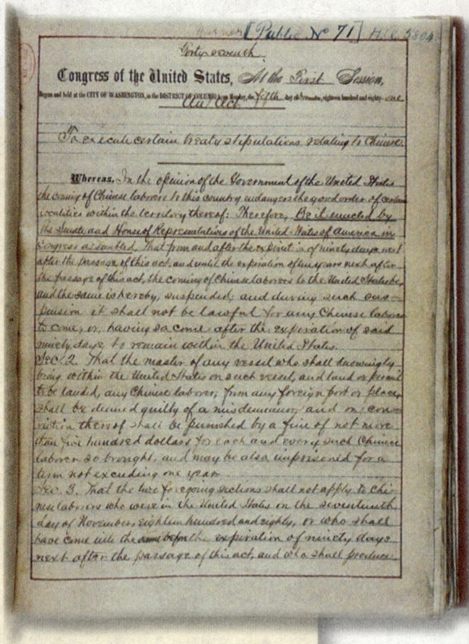

Learn More A document called an *act* is an official law that has been passed by a government. The Chinese Exclusion Act of 1882 stopped Chinese worker immigration to the United States. This was the first major act in U.S. history to limit the immigration of free people. It also excluded Chinese immigrants from becoming U.S. citizens. Read the introduction to the act below. Then answer the questions.

"Be it enacted [made into law] by the Senate and House of Representatives of the United States of America in Congress assembled, That from and after the expiration [end] of ninety days next after the passage of this act, and until the expiration of ten years next after the passage of this act, the coming of Chinese laborers [workers] to the United States be, and the same is hereby, suspended [stopped]; and during such suspension it shall not be lawful for any Chinese laborer to come, or, having so come after the expiration of said ninety days, to remain within the United States."

1. **Circle the words in the document's introduction that mean "something comes to an end."** Apply

2. **Why do you think Congress passed this act? Do you think this act was fair?** Analyze

____

____

____

____

____

____

____

Name:

H-SS 4.4.4 Describe rapid American immigration, internal migration, settlement, and the growth of towns and cities (e.g., Los Angeles).

Lesson 4

How have immigration and settlement helped California grow?

SET THE SCENE In the early 1900s, California's population continued to rise. Even more people came here from all over the world. Many of them hoped to find jobs in our state's many new factories and on big farms. How did all these new people change California?

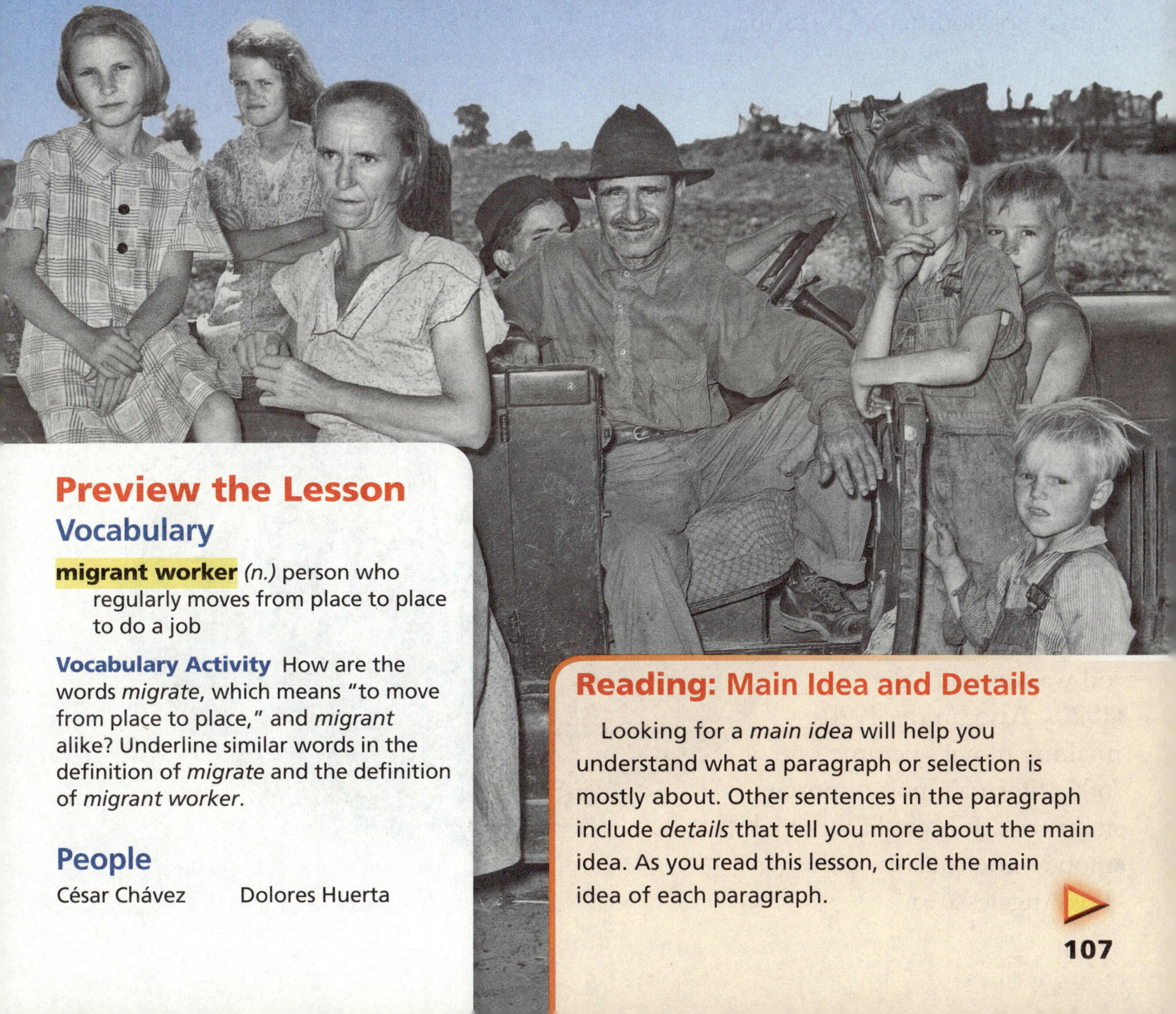

Preview the Lesson

Vocabulary

migrant worker *(n.)* person who regularly moves from place to place to do a job

Vocabulary Activity How are the words *migrate*, which means "to move from place to place," and *migrant* alike? Underline similar words in the definition of *migrate* and the definition of *migrant worker*.

People

César Chávez   Dolores Huerta

Reading: Main Idea and Details

Looking for a *main idea* will help you understand what a paragraph or selection is mostly about. Other sentences in the paragraph include *details* that tell you more about the main idea. As you read this lesson, circle the main idea of each paragraph.

Population Growth in the 1900s

California's population grew quickly in the first half of the 1900s. It grew from 1.5 million in 1900 to 5.7 million in 1930. This growth happened for several reasons. First, the cost of train travel dropped. This made travel to California much cheaper. In the early 1900s, automobiles became very important. As many people traveled to California in cars, our state's population rose even more. People came here for jobs, but some also came for the warm, sunny climate of Southern California.

1. Why did California grow so quickly during the early 1900s? *Main Idea and Details*

Growth of Los Angeles

Los Angeles also had a huge population boom in the early 1900s. Its population in 1930 was about 1.2 million, more than ten times larger than it had been in 1900. This increase was caused by economic growth in several different areas. One area was farming. Farming grew because irrigation allowed farmers to grow crops in the desert areas of Southern California. Another area of economic growth was the oil industry. Oil was found in Southern California in the 1890s. Even more oil was found in the 1920s. Also, in the 1920s, making movies became one of California's most important industries. It brought more jobs, money, and tourists to the Los Angeles area.

2. Underline in the text what caused the population boom in the Los Angeles area in the early 1900s. *Cause and Effect*

Motion pictures have been filmed in California since the early 1900s.

Migrant workers often move from farm to farm to harvest the crops that are in season.

Workers on Large Farms

California has many large farms that use **migrant workers,** or people who regularly move from place to place to do a job. Without their help, many California farmers might not be able to afford to manage large farms. When the citrus industry began in the late 1800s, many Chinese, and later Japanese and Mexicans, worked for low pay in citrus groves, or tree farms.

In the 1960s, leaders named César Chávez and Dolores Huerta demanded better pay and working conditions for migrant workers. They organized laborers, or workers, to join together and fight for these changes. For example, a group of grape pickers held a strike to improve their working conditions. Efforts such as these helped people across the country learn about the unfair treatment of migrant workers.

3. How have migrant workers impacted the citrus industry in California?

Main Idea and Details

Summary

Several developments caused the population of California to boom in the 1900s. Why did many people come to California in the first half of the 1900s?

Biography

César Chávez, 1927–1993
Dolores Huerta, b. 1930

Learn More César Chávez spent most of his life around migrant workers. His family worked on farms, causing him to move often. As a result, he could not always attend school. Chávez joined the U.S. Navy as a teenager. After his service ended, he returned to migrant farm work. He later focused on improving the lives of migrant workers. His work earned him the Presidential Medal of Freedom.

Dolores Huerta also wanted to make life better for farm workers. Her father had been a migrant worker. Huerta and Chávez started the National Farm Workers Association (NFWA) in 1962, which later became part of the United Farm Workers of America (UFW). The NFWA gave farm workers more power. They gained better pay and working conditions by standing up to farm owners together.

Use the text to answer the questions below.

1. **Underline what César Chávez and Dolores Huerta did together.** *Identify*

2. **How did the NFWA help farm workers?** *Analyze*

____

____

____

____

Name:

H-SS 4.4.5 Discuss the effects of the Great Depression, the Dust Bowl, and World War II on California.

Lesson 5

What was California's role in the twentieth century?

SET THE SCENE The first half of the 1900s was a time of great change in the United States. During the 1920s, businesses grew and jobs were plentiful. However, the Great Depression and World War II brought hard times in the 1930s and 1940s. How did these events affect California?

Preview the Lesson

Vocabulary

stock market *(n.)* the business of buying and selling shares of companies

depression *(n.)* a period when there is little business activity and many people do not have jobs

drought *(n.)* a long period of time without rain

inflation *(n.)* when prices rise

ration *(v.)* to allow people only a limited amount of something because there is not enough of it

Vocabulary Activity Write the vocabulary word from the list above that best completes the sentence below.

The plants dried up and turned brown during the ______________.

People

Franklin D. Roosevelt

Reading: Cause and Effect

As you read, ask yourself questions to help you understand what makes things happen: *What caused this to happen? What happened as a result of the event?* On page 112, circle these cause-and-effect signal words and phrases: *as a result, so,* and *caused.*

1920 1925

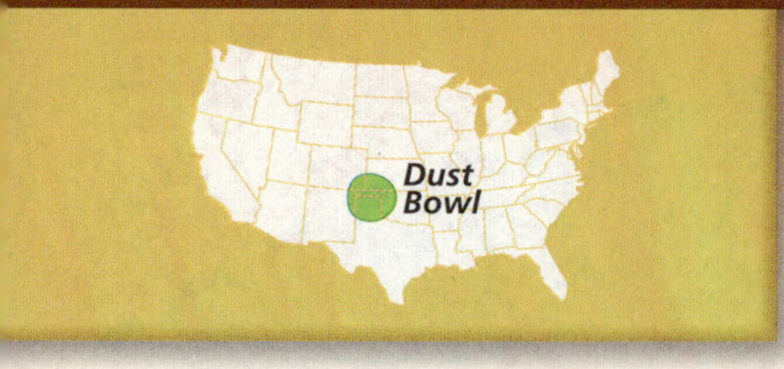

Hard Times Across the Country

Americans had enjoyed the growth of businesses and jobs in the 1920s. But the good times of the 1920s soon changed to hard times. In 1929 the stock market failed. The **stock market** is the business of buying and selling shares of companies. That failure marked the beginning of the Great Depression. A **depression** is a period when there is little business activity and many people do not have jobs. Across the nation, businesses and banks had to close. Some people lost their jobs, savings, farms, and homes. Prices fell, so it cost farmers more to harvest crops than the crops were worth. As a result, many fruit and vegetable crops were not harvested and rotted in fields.

The lack of jobs caused conflicts among Californians. Some people blamed the hard times on immigrants. They felt the immigrants were taking their jobs. So the state forced many people from Mexico and other countries to leave.

1. How did the Great Depression affect life in California and the United States?

Cause and Effect

Millions of people lost their jobs in the Great Depression.

During the Great Depression, many farms, such as this one in Idaho, failed and were abandoned.

1930

1935

1929 The stock market crash marks the beginning of the Great Depression.

1930s Drought in the Southwest and parts of the Midwest creates the Dust Bowl.

Searching for a Better Life

In the 1930s, more than one million people from other parts of the country came to California. They thought they could find jobs and a better life here.

Many of these people came west as a result of a bad drought in parts of the Midwest and Southwest. A **drought** is a long period of time without rain. The drought created an area called the Dust Bowl in parts of Colorado, Kansas, New Mexico, Oklahoma, and Texas. High winds caused huge dust storms in these areas. The soil was so dry from the drought that it blew off the farm fields, filled the air, and settled back down in thick layers. As a result of the drought farmers could not grow crops. Many farm machines were ruined, and some animals died.

Many Dust Bowl farmers had to leave their homes. Thousands of families packed up their belongings and moved to California. Most of these people could find jobs only as migrant workers, picking crops for low pay.

2. How did the Dust Bowl impact population growth in California? Use details from the text to support your answer. *Main Idea and Details*

Families from Dust Bowl states often came to California hoping to find jobs and a better life.

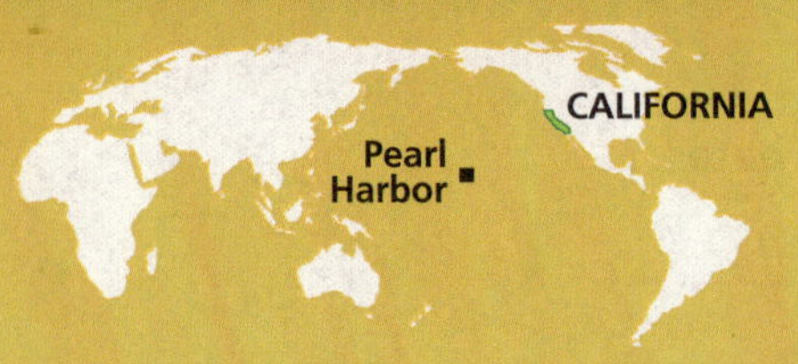

1939

California's Wartime Workers

After years of hard times, the Great Depression in the United States came to an end. In 1939 World War II began in Europe. When the United States entered the war in 1941, war supplies were needed. President Franklin D. Roosevelt asked the U.S. government to spend large amounts of money on these supplies. This spending helped create new jobs.

California workers in aircraft plants and shipyards were a big help to our country during World War II. California's sunny weather made it the perfect place to test airplanes. Also, the San Francisco Bay area became one of the largest shipbuilding centers in the world. Workers at the Mare Island Naval Shipyard built submarines, battleships, and other ships.

Wartime Hardships

Hundreds of thousands of people moved to California to take wartime jobs in the early 1940s. But the sudden population boom caused some hardships. Schools were overcrowded. A number of goods were in short supply due to the war, including meat, cheese, coffee, sugar, tires, and gasoline. Inflation also grew. **Inflation** is when prices rise. To slow down inflation, the government rationed some goods, such as butter and gasoline. To **ration** is to allow people only a limited amount of something because there is not enough of it.

3. How did California help the country during World War II?
Main Idea and Details

Many California women went to work in factories, helping build planes for the war.

4. What caused the government to decide to ration goods?
Cause and Effect

1945 1950

1941 The United States enters World War II after the Japanese bomb Pearl Harbor.

1945 World War II ends.

Japanese Americans often built rock gardens at internment camps.

During World War II, entire families of Japanese Americans were held in camps like this one at Manzanar, California.

Internment Camps

World War II had other negative effects on life in California. On December 7, 1941, Japanese planes bombed U.S. Navy ships in Pearl Harbor in Hawaii. As a result, the United States declared war on Japan. Some people were afraid that Japanese and Japanese Americans in the United States would support Japan in the war. President Roosevelt ordered about 120,000 Japanese and Japanese Americans who were living in California and other western states to be sent to internment camps. An internment camp is a place where people are held against their will, often during a war.

Two internment camps in California were the Tule Lake War Relocation Center near the Oregon border and the Manzanar War Relocation Center near Independence. More than 18,000 people were held at Tule. Another 11,000 were held at Manzanar. The camps were surrounded by barbed wire and guard towers. Many of the people in the camps were U.S. citizens. By the time they were released in 1945, when the war ended, most had lost the homes and businesses they owned before the war.

5. In the text, circle the negative effects that the internment camps had on the lives of Japanese and Japanese Americans in California.

Main Idea and Details

Summary

Major events in the United States in the 1900s had a big impact on life in our state. Name three events that happened in the United States in the first half of the 1900s and tell how they affected life in California.

Susan Ahn Cuddy, b. 1915

Learn More Susan Ahn Cuddy considers herself both Korean and American. She was born in Los Angeles in 1915, but her parents were born in Korea. She is proud of both cultures. She always remembers what her father told her: "Be a good American. Do your best . . . and don't forget your heritage."

During World War II, Cuddy became one of the first Asian Americans in the U.S. Navy. When she first tried to enter the Navy, she was not accepted. But she did not give up and was eventually allowed in the service. In the Navy, she used her language skills to gather information to help fight the war. After the war, she worked for the National Security Agency, which handles secret codes.

Answer the questions below.

1. **Circle in the text what Cuddy is best known for doing.** *Identify*
2. **Why do you think Cuddy is a good role model?** *Analyze*

____

____

____

____

____

Name:

H-SS 4.4.6 Describe the development and locations of new industries since the nineteenth century, such as the aerospace industry, electronics industry, large-scale commercial agriculture and irrigation projects, the oil and automobile industries, communications and defense industries, and important trade links with the Pacific Basin.

Lesson 6

What new industries came to California in the twentieth century?

CONNECT TO YOU You might have a computer in your classroom or at home. You've probably seen jet airplanes flying overhead. You may often see people using cell phones. Fifty years ago, these things were not as common or did not even exist. Today, our state is a leader in making all of these things.

Preview the Lesson

Vocabulary

aerospace *(n.)* the science of flight

aqueduct *(n.)* a pipe or other system that brings water from a distance

Vocabulary Activity Look for word parts to help figure out the meaning of words. Circle the word part from the list above that means "water."

Reading: Cause and Effect

Writers use causes and effects to help readers see connections between events. A *cause* tells why something happens. An *effect* tells what happens as a result. As you read page 118, underline one of the effects that little rain had on farms in Southern California.

California's Biggest Industries

The airplane, computer, communications, and agricultural industries are all important to California. As you have learned, our state's aircraft industry grew during World War II. In the late 1950s, the United States began to explore space. California became the leader in the aerospace industry. **Aerospace** is the science of flight. Today, California's biggest industry is the production of electronics, including cell phones, televisions, and stereos. This also includes computers for homes and offices and electronics for aircraft and military vehicles.

California also leads the United States in crop production, especially in fruit and nuts. In fact, our state is the sixth largest agricultural exporter in the world. California has more than 50,000 farms, but much of our farmland does not get enough rain. Aqueducts are used to bring water to our farmland. An **aqueduct** is a pipe or other system that brings water from a distance.

1. Sequence **Use sequence words to describe how the aerospace industry has grown since World War II.**

Industry	General Location
Aerospace	Southern California
Communication	Northern and Southern California
Electronics	Northern California
Large-scale Commercial Agriculture	Central and Southern California
Military/Defense	Northern and Southern California
Oil and Automobile	Southern California

The Los Angeles Aqueduct is a system of pipes that brings water from Owens Valley to Los Angeles.

Oil and Automobiles

Oil is also important to California's economy. California's first oil boom was in the 1860s, and then oil was discovered near Los Angeles in 1892. As a result, many oil companies were formed in our state between 1890 and 1900.

In the early 1900s, automobiles became more affordable and popular. Cars and trucks made it easier for people to move goods, drive to work, and travel. But this meant that people needed even more oil and gasoline. Another big oil boom came in the 1920s in Los Angeles. This oil boom helped California's economy grow.

2. How did cars and trucks affect California? *Cause and Effect*

Trade with the Pacific Basin

Another important part of California's economy is its trade with other countries. Much of this trade is done with the Pacific Basin region, which includes countries located on the coasts along the Pacific Ocean. California exports food and electronic goods to Asian countries such as Japan, South Korea, Taiwan, and Singapore.

3. Underline details in the text about the Pacific Basin. *Main Idea and Details*

The Pacific Basin

Draw lines from California to some of the Asian countries it trades with.

Summary

Many industries in California have been growing throughout the 1900s. Name two of California's top industries and list two facts about each one.

Biography

California Women in Space

Learn More

Sally Ride, b. 1951

Sally Ride was born in Los Angeles. As an adult, Ride became an astronaut with the National Aeronautics and Space Administration (NASA). On June 18, 1983, she rode on the shuttle *Challenger* and became the first American woman in space. Ride now teaches physics to college students.

Ellen Ochoa, b. 1958

Like Ride, Ellen Ochoa is from Los Angeles. She received an advanced degree from Stanford University in 1985 and became an astronaut with NASA in July 1991. Ochoa has spent more than 900 hours in space.

Patricia Cowings, b. 1948

Patricia Cowings also works at NASA. She trained to be an astronaut but has never gone into space. Cowings does research at NASA. She helps astronauts adapt to the special conditions of space.

Use the text to answer the questions below.

1. **In the text, circle the names of the two women who still work at NASA.** *Identify*

2. **What questions would you ask Sally Ride and Ellen Ochoa about being in space?** *Pose Questions*

Name:

H-SS 4.4.7 Trace the evolution of California's water system into a network of dams, aqueducts, and reservoirs.

Lesson 7

How did California's water system develop?

CONNECT TO YOU It's nice to know that you have fresh, clean water when you turn on the faucet. But making sure that we have enough clean water has been a big challenge in our state. How has our state managed its water system?

Preview the Lesson

Vocabulary

reservoir *(n.)* a place where water is collected and stored for use

delta *(n.)* an area of land where a river separates into smaller rivers flowing into a body of water

bay *(n.)* a part of a sea or lake that cuts into a coastline

renewable resource *(n.)* a resource that can be replaced

nonrenewable resource *(n.)* a resource that comes from the earth and cannot be replaced

Vocabulary Activity Look for word parts to help figure out the meaning of words. Circle the root word in *renewable* above. Underline the prefix and the suffix.

Reading: Sequence

Reading Skill

Looking for important dates and time-order words will help you keep track of a sequence of events. As you read page 122, circle details that help you follow important developments in California's water systems.

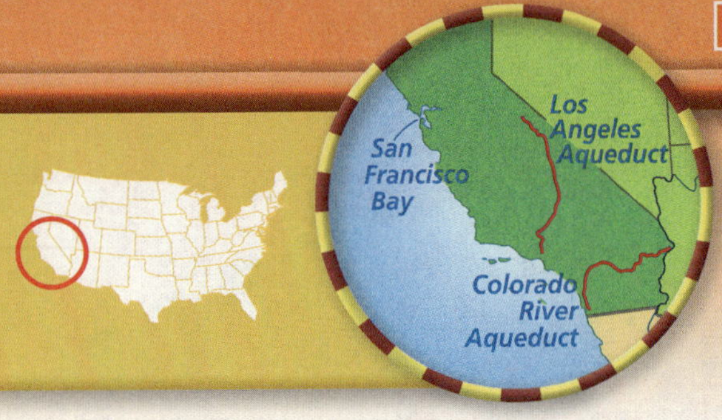

1910 1920 1930

1913

Dams, Aqueducts, and Reservoirs

California has made a big effort to get water to the southern part of the state. A large part of our state's population lives in that area, which is usually hot and dry. But most of the available water is in the northern part of California. To get water to the south, California has built dams, aqueducts, and reservoirs. A **reservoir** is a place where water is collected and stored for use.

Many of the state's water projects now provide water to the dry parts of California. First, in 1913 the Los Angeles Aqueduct began bringing water to Los Angeles. The Colorado River Aqueduct later brought water to coastal cities, including San Diego in 1941. More recently, the California Aqueduct started delivering water to Southern California in 1973. Today, it serves two-thirds of the people in that area.

Construction on the Hoover Dam began in 1931 to bring water to parts of Southern California.

1. Sequence **List California's aqueducts in the order in which they were completed.**

Circle the aqueduct that brings water to San Diego from the Colorado River.

1940 1950 1960 1970

1941 The Colorado River Aqueduct begins bringing water to coastal cities.

1973 The California Aqueduct begins bringing water from the San Francisco Bay area to Southern California.

1936 The Hoover Dam is completed on the Colorado River.

The Central Valley Project

Getting water to the central coast area of the state is also important. Construction on the Central Valley Project began in the 1930s. It is made up of many dams, canals, and reservoirs that provide water for irrigation. Some of the water comes from the delta of the Sacramento and San Joaquin Rivers. A **delta** is an area of land where a river separates into smaller rivers flowing into a body of water. These rivers empty into San Francisco Bay. A **bay** is a part of a sea or lake that cuts into a coastline.

Water Resources

California gets some of its electricity from hydroelectric power plants. The plants use the energy of moving water to make electricity. Hydroelectric power is a **renewable resource,** which is a resource that can be replaced. Hydroelectric plants help us save nonrenewable resources, such as coal and oil. A **nonrenewable resource** is a resource that comes from the earth and cannot be replaced.

California still has periods of drought. That is why it is important to conserve, or save, water. Some things you can do to save water are turning off the water while you are brushing your teeth and taking quicker showers. Also, do not play with the water hose or sprinkler. Making sure you do not waste water helps keep California from using up all of its water supply.

2. What is the Central Valley Project? Why is it important?
Evaluate

3. Underline in the text an important difference between a renewable and a nonrenewable resource.
Compare and Contrast

Summary

Water is an important resource. It needs to be managed carefully in California so we do not run out of it. How has California met its water needs?

Skill

Cross-Section Diagrams

Learn More A cross-section diagram shows a "slice" of something. It cuts through an object so that you can see how it looks on the inside. Below is a cross-section diagram of a dam and hydroelectric power plant. It will help you understand how many dams work. Use the diagram below to answer the following questions.

Try It

1. **Draw a line that traces the path of water through a hydroelectric power plant.** *Analyze*

2. **The reservoir holds water for the hydroelectric plant to use. What would happen if it were empty?** *Analyze*

____

____

3. **A dam is just one object that a cross-section diagram might help explain. Name something else that could be explained using a cross-section diagram.** *Apply*

____

____

Name:

H-SS 4.4.8 Describe the history and development of California's public education system, including universities and community colleges.

Lesson 8

How did California's education system develop?

CONNECT TO YOU Today, you are a student in a California elementary school. Soon you will go to middle school or junior high, and then on to high school. After that you might continue your education or you may decide to do something else. How did California create its system of schools?

Preview the Lesson

Vocabulary

public *(adj.)* available for anyone to use

private *(adj.)* not owned by the government

trade school *(n.)* a place where people learn how to do a job

college *(n.)* a school where people study after high school

university *(n.)* the highest level of school from which you can earn a degree

degree *(n.)* a rank or title given to someone who has completed a program of study at a school

Vocabulary Activity Write the vocabulary word from the list above that best completes the sentence below.

She received her ________ in biology after completing the program in four years.

Reading: Sequence

Reading Skill

Sometimes writers provide details to help you follow the order of events, such as dates and time-order words. As you read the lesson, circle details that help you keep track of important events about California's school system.

This photo shows an early school in Shasta City, California.

California's First Schools

Education is very important to Californians. One of the earliest schools in California was started in Santa Clara by Olive Isbell in 1846. At that time the area was still a territory of Mexico. When California became a state in 1850, the first public school opened, in San Francisco. **Public** means available for anyone to use. In 1874 the state passed a law that said that all children must have an elementary education.

California Schools Today

California has thousands of public high schools and elementary schools. These schools are provided by the state government and are managed by the state Board of Education, which is part of the California Department of Education. The Department of Education decides how government money will be shared among the many schools. California also has private schools. A **private** school is one that is not owned by the government. Private schools may charge money in order for students to attend.

1. Sequence **Describe two important historical events with their dates that led to the development of California's school system.**

2. List similarities and differences between public and private schools.
Compare and Contrast

Education After High School

Some people choose to get more education after high school. Some of them go to a **trade school** to learn how to do a job. Some go to community colleges, where students usually take classes for two years. A **college** is a school where people study after high school. Most of the state's community colleges are part of the California Community College system. This system has more than 100 colleges.

California Universities and Colleges

California also has two larger public school systems that students can attend for four or more years. These are the California State University (CSU) system and the University of California (UC) system. A **university** is the highest level of school from which you can earn a degree. A **degree** is a rank or title given to someone who completes a program of study at a school.

In 1862 California's first state college opened in San Francisco. It moved to San Jose in 1871. It became the first school in the CSU system and is now called San Jose State University. In 1868 the first school in the UC system opened in Oakland. It later moved to Berkeley and became UC Berkeley.

Today, California's system of public colleges and universities is the largest in the country. There are more than thirty public universities in California. Our state has many private colleges and universities as well.

3. What choices do people have after high school if they want to get more education?
Main Idea and Details

4. Underline details in the text about California's two public university systems.
Main Ideas and Details

UC Berkeley is the oldest school in the University of California system.

Summary

There are many different ways that students of all ages can get an education in California. Describe California's school system today.

Skill

Revising and Editing

Learn More Good writers revise and edit their work in order to improve it. When writers revise their work, they add, delete, or rearrange text. When they edit, they correct mistakes in spelling, grammar, and punctuation. Writers often use special proofreading marks when they edit.

Try It

The first paragraph to the right has been edited using the proofreading marks below. Review the proofreading marks and the edited paragraph. Then read the second paragraph. Use the proofreading marks to revise and edit the paragraph.

sp	**for spelling error**
(delete mark)	**to delete**
∧	**to insert new text or punctuation**
≡	**to capitalize**
⊙	**period**

Mrs olive Isbell started one of the earliest schools in the California territory in 1846. The skool was in an old stable near the Santa clara mission Their were hardly any books. The classroom did not have chalkboards, paper, or pencils. Mrs. Isbell used charcoal to write letters of the alphabit on her students' hands.

Two years later San Franciso had its first school. The school was located on on portsmouth Square. Six weeks later school closed because Thomas Dale, its founder, went off to find gold. In 1850 the sity of San francisco passed a city law establishing free public schools

Name:

H-SS 4.4.9 Analyze the impact of twentieth-century Californians on the nation's artistic and cultural development, including the rise of the entertainment industry (e.g., Louis B. Mayer, Walt Disney, John Steinbeck, Ansel Adams, Dorothea Lange, John Wayne).

Lesson 9

How have Californians made our state unique?

CONNECT TO YOU What is your favorite movie or television show? It may have been made by a company in California. Our state is known for its movie and television industries. What other kinds of arts and entertainment have been produced in California?

Preview the Lesson

Vocabulary

culture *(n.)* the customs, arts, entertainment, and recreation of a group

actor *(n.)* a person who performs in plays, movies, or television shows

Vocabulary Activity Underline the word above that might include photographs and popular music.

People

Louis B. Mayer
Walt Disney
John Wayne
Ansel Adams
Dorothea Lange
Jack London
John Steinbeck

Reading: Fact and Opinion

A *fact* is a statement that is generally believed to be true. An *opinion* is a person's belief or judgment. Learning how to identify a fact and opinion can help you evaluate information found in nonfiction texts. As you read the first paragraph on page 130, underline facts in the text about Louis B. Mayer.

Movies Come to California

The Los Angeles area has been one of the world's biggest motion-picture centers since the early 1900s. In 1911 the Nestor Company built the first movie studio in Hollywood. Southern California's mild, sunny weather allowed filmmakers to work outdoors almost year-round. In the 1930s and 1940s, movie studios were run by powerful businessmen, such as Louis B. Mayer. He helped start the Metro-Goldwyn-Mayer studio, which is known as MGM.

1. List two facts about the entertainment industry.
Fact and Opinion

The Entertainment Industry Today

The entertainment industry is still an important part of California's economy. Hundreds of thousands of people are involved in the production of films, television shows, commercials, music, and video and computer games. Millions of tourists come to the Los Angeles area to see how movies are made. Amusement parks in California also attract many visitors.

2. Why do you think the entertainment industry is important to California?
Draw Conclusions

Not only do Californians enjoy our state's amusement parks, but the parks also bring many tourists to California.

California and the Arts

In the last century, many Californians helped shape American culture. **Culture** is the customs, arts, entertainment, and recreation of a group. Walt Disney created many cartoon characters and opened Disneyland in 1955. The film actor John Wayne is famous for starring in movies from the 1920s through the 1970s. An **actor** is a person who performs in plays, movies, or television shows.

Famous California photographers such as Ansel Adams and Dorothea Lange captured images of our state. Adams is well known for his photos of Yosemite National Park. Lange's photos taken during the Great Depression and in the Dust Bowl showed the hardships that many people faced.

Jack London and John Steinbeck were both famous California writers. London's novels include *Call of the Wild* (1903) and *White Fang* (1906). Steinbeck's most famous novel, *The Grapes of Wrath* (1939), follows the struggles of a poor Dust Bowl family seeking a better life in California. Several of Steinbeck's books are set in California, but London's novels take place all over the world.

3. List one Californian who helped shape American culture. Explain why this person is important.
Main Idea and Details

Dorthea Lange photographed Californians during the Great Depression, such as this mother with her children.

John Wayne *(left)* was famous for his roles in westerns, or movies that were set in the West.

Summary

Our state has also played a big role in twentieth-century American culture through arts and entertainment. How is California's arts and entertainment industry important to the state's economy?

Biography

George Lucas, b. 1944
Steven Spielberg, b. 1947

Learn More George Lucas and Steven Spielberg are important in today's film industry. They have both made movies that use impressive special effects. Each has won an Academy Award for his life's work. George Lucas grew up in Modesto, California. He studied filmmaking at the University of Southern California. One of his early movies was *THX 1138*. He later used the title *THX* for a high-quality sound system he helped develop. Lucas went on to write, film, and produce the *Star Wars* movies.

Steven Spielberg has been making movies since he was a child. He won a filmmaking contest at age thirteen, but he was not accepted into film school. He did not give up, and he continued to make films. One of his early films was called *Amblin*. *Amblin* later became the name of his production company that made his films *E.T.—the Extraterrestrial* and *Jurassic Park*.

Lucas and Spielberg have also worked together. The *Indiana Jones* movies were produced by Lucas and directed by Spielberg.

George Lucas

Steven Spielberg

Answer the questions below.

1. **Circle the movies that George Lucas has made. Underline the movies that Steven Spielberg has made. On the line below, write the movie series that they made together.** *Identify*

____

2. **Why do you think Spielberg named his production company after one of his early films?** *Analyze*

____

Name:

Unit 5

Study Journal

In this unit you will learn about how the United States and California Constitutions shape our state and our nation. You will also see how different levels and branches of government affect your life every day. Complete the activities on these pages as you read the unit.

What I know about . . .

the United States and California governments:

What are the branches and levels of government?

Fill in the duties of the three branches of government in the boxes below.

Legislative	Executive	Judicial

Fill in the boxes below with the responsibilities of each level of government.

Federal	State	Local

Complete these sections as you read the unit.

Name one right that comes with citizenship in either California or the United States. Then name at least one duty of citizenship.

Right

____

____

Duty

____

____

In which type of local government would you most like to participate? Circle it below and then write two facts about it.

- City or town
- County
- School district
- Rancheria or reservation

1. ______________________

____

2. ______________________

____

List the important federal and state documents that were approved in the years shown below.

1776 ______________________

1788 ______________________

1791 ______________________

1849 ______________________

1879 ______________________

I have learned . . .

____

Name:

H-SS 4.5.1 Discuss what the U.S. Constitution is and why it is important (i.e., a written document that defines the structure and purpose of the U.S. government and describes the shared powers of federal, state, and local governments).

Why was the United States Constitution created?

SET THE SCENE When you play a game with your friends, who decides what the rules are and whether or not they are fair? More than two hundred years ago, the founders of the United States met in order to write a constitution, or a plan for the government of a country. What rules for the new country did the U.S. Constitution include?

Preview the Lesson

Vocabulary

convention *(n.)* a large meeting arranged for a special purpose

principle *(n.)* an important belief

amendment *(n.)* a change or addition

responsibility *(n.)* a duty or something that must be done

Vocabulary Activity Circle the vocabulary word in the list above that best completes this sentence: *The founders of the United States held a* ______________ *in order to write the Constitution.*

Reading: Fact and Opinion

A *fact* is something that is generally believed to be true. An *opinion* is a person's belief or judgment. As you read page 136, underline the opinions of the representatives.

1775 1780

1776 The Declaration of Independence is written.

A New Government

The United States was not created all at once. In 1776 the Declaration of Independence was written. It stated that American colonists wanted to be free from Great Britain. After the colonists fought and won a war against Britain, they had to decide what kind of government their new nation would have. In 1787 representatives from the states held a convention in Philadelphia, Pennsylvania. A **convention** is a large meeting arranged for a special purpose. The purpose of this convention was to create the new government.

At the convention, the representatives did not agree on the structure of the new government. Some of them believed that it would be best to have one strong central government with most of the power over all the states. Others felt that it would be better to give the individual states more control. In the end, the representatives decided on a federal system, in which power is shared between the states and the central government. The U.S. Constitution was ratified, or approved, in 1788.

1. Fact and Opinion **List two facts that support the following statement: The United States faced many challenges in becoming an independent country.**

The Constitutional Convention of 1787 was held in Independence Hall in Philadelphia, Pennsylvania.

1785 1790 1795

1788

1791 The Bill of Rights is ratified.

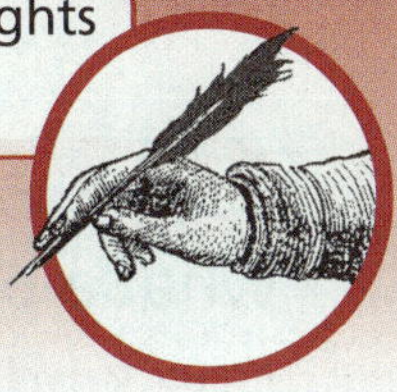

Changes to the Constitution

The Constitution describes the structure for the government. It reflects the **principles,** or important beliefs, of the people of the United States. One important fact about the Constitution is that it can be changed. These changes or additions are called **amendments.** The first ten amendments were ratified in 1791. They are known as the Bill of Rights, and they protect the rights and freedoms of all U.S. citizens.

2. Why do you think it is important that the Constitution can be amended? *Draw Conclusions*

Three Levels of Government

The Constitution makes laws and provides services for the people of all states. Local, state, and federal governments share power. Each level has different responsibilities. A **responsibility** is a duty or something that must be done. Local governments make laws and provide services for towns and cities. State governments do the same types of jobs for an entire state. The federal government handles laws and services for the people of all the states.

3. In the text, circle the responsibilities of the federal government. *Main Idea and Details*

Although Yosemite is in California, it is run by the federal government because it is a national park.

Summary

The early leaders of our country wrote the Constitution to lay out the structure and purpose for the government. How is the U.S. Constitution important today?

Primary Source

Documents: The Bill of Rights

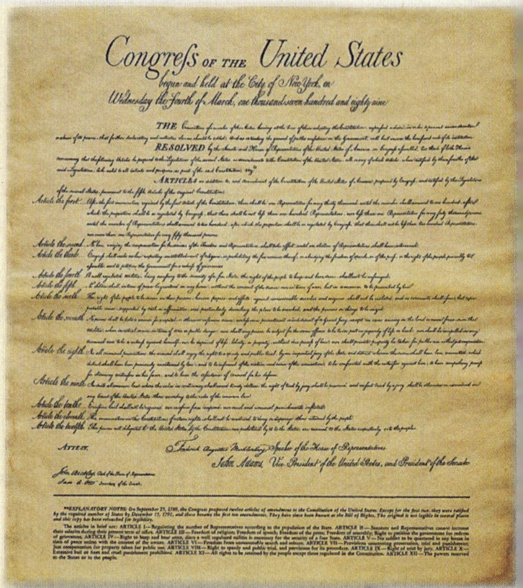

Learn More You have already learned what a primary source is. Documents are one kind of primary source. They usually include official information. As you have learned, the Bill of Rights is the first ten amendments to the U.S. Constitution.

When the Constitution was written in 1787, it did not include the Bill of Rights. Many Americans had just fought the American Revolution to gain their freedom from Britain. Some Americans were worried that the new government might try to limit some freedoms. As a result, the Bill of Rights was written. It protects certain rights and freedoms. For example, the Sixth Amendment states that people have a right to a trial by jury and to a lawyer in criminal cases.

The First Amendment protects the freedom of religion, freedom of speech, freedom of the press, the right to assemble peacefully, and the right to voice complaints to the government.

1. Circle two of the freedoms above that are important to you. *Identify*

2. Explain how one of these freedoms is important in your life. *Apply*

____

____

____

First Amendment

Congress shall make no law respecting an establishment of religion, or prohibiting the free exercise thereof; or abridging the freedom of speech, or of the press; or the right of the people peaceably to assemble, and to petition the Government for a redress of grievances.

Name:

H-SS 4.5.2 Understand the purpose of the California Constitution, its key principles, and its relationship to the U.S. Constitution.

Lesson 2

How does the California Constitution affect you?

CONNECT TO YOU Why do you think we need a constitution for our state? You know that the U.S. Constitution protects the freedoms of all U.S. citizens. In the same way, the California Constitution protects the rights of Californians. How do you think it affects you?

Preview the Lesson

Vocabulary

citizenship *(n.)* the duties, rights, and responsibilities of individuals living in a state or country

Vocabulary Activity Look for word parts that help you figure out the meaning of words. Circle the root word above in *citizenship* and underline its suffix.

Reading: Main Idea and Details

Identifying the main idea will help you understand what a paragraph or selection is mostly about. Other sentences will include details that support the main idea. As you read page 140, underline the main idea in the second paragraph.

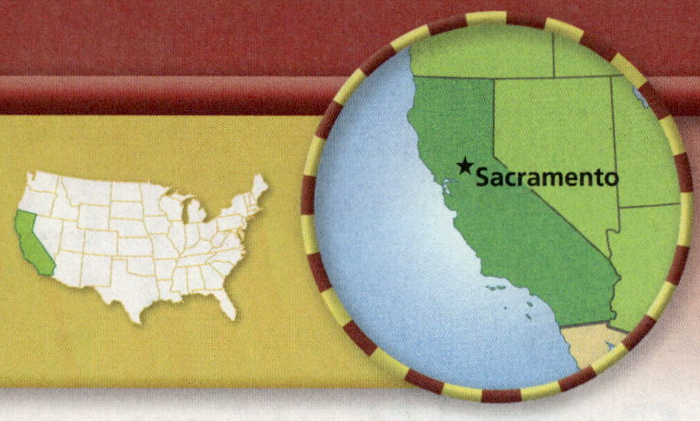

1850 | 1855 | 1860

1849 California's first constitution is written.

1850 California becomes a state.

1854 Sacramento becomes the state capital.

Two Constitutions

The California Constitution and the U.S. Constitution are alike in many ways. Both are plans for governing people. Both begin with a short preamble, or introduction. Articles, or sections, follow the preamble. Both constitutions give people the right to freedom and to choose their representatives.

Our state's and country's constitutions are different as well. The California Constitution describes the laws of our state. The articles of the state constitution explain the rights of California citizens. They also set up three branches of state government. The California Constitution covers such topics as voting, education, and how the state spends money. The U.S. Constitution describes the responsibilities of the federal government. This includes defending our country, printing money, and making agreements with other nations.

1. Use the details in the chart below to help you determine the main idea of the first paragraph. *Main Idea and Details*

Main Idea

[ ]

Detail: plan to govern people

Detail: grouped into articles

Detail: right to live in freedom

Detail: choose representatives

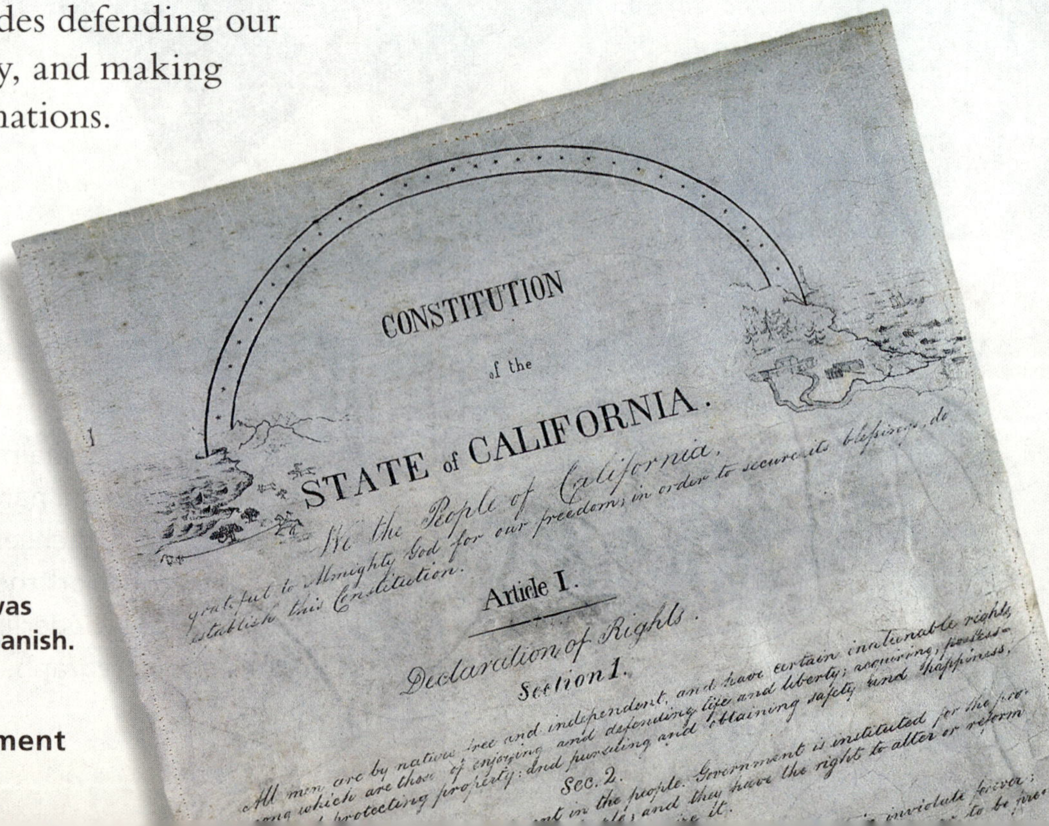

California's first constitution was written in both English and Spanish.

1865 | 1870 | 1875 | 1880

1879

These California citizens are fulfilling their responsibility to vote.

The California Constitution

California has had two state constitutions. The first was written in 1849 and approved by the U.S. government in 1850. At that point, California became a state. Sacramento became the state capital in 1854. In 1879 a second constitution was approved. This is the one we use today. It explains what it means to be a citizen of our state.

Citizenship includes the duties, rights, and responsibilities of an individual living in a state or country. Our state constitution says that all California citizens are free and have rights that cannot be taken away. These rights include the freedom to enjoy and defend their lives and liberty. Citizens also have the right to buy, own, and protect their property.

California citizens have responsibilities and duties as well. It is important for citizens to learn about the government, vote, and obey the laws. Citizens should help their community and speak up about matters that are important to them.

2. What is the purpose of the California Constitution?
Main Ideas and Details

Summary

Both the U.S. Constitution and the California Constitution protect the rights of citizens. Summarize the responsibilities of a California citizen.

Primary Source

Symbols: State Seal

Learn More Every state in the United States has a state seal. A seal is usually a circle-shaped image that represents, or stands for, a state or a country. California's seal was designed in 1849 while California was in the process of becoming a state. Robert Sheldon Garnett created the seal, and Caleb Lyon presented the idea for it to the constitutional convention. The convention approved the seal.

Here are some of the symbols you can find on the Great Seal of California and what they stand for:

1. **Thirty-one stars** represent the thirty-one states in the United States in 1850, including California.
2. A **gold miner** represents the wealth and opportunity that California had to offer.
3. The word ***Eureka*** is Greek for "I have found it!" This most likely refers to the miners finding gold.
4. A **grizzly bear** represents California's agriculture and wildlife.

Use the seal at right to answer the questions below.

1. On the seal, write the number of each item (above) on the part of the seal that it describes. *Identify*

2. If you were creating a seal for your classroom, what symbols would you include? *Apply*

____

____

____

Name:

H-SS 4.5.3 Describe the similarities (e.g., written documents, rule of law, consent of the governed, three separate branches) and differences (e.g., scope of jurisdiction, limits on government powers, use of the military) among federal, state, and local governments.

Lesson 3

How are federal, state, and local governments alike and different?

CONNECT TO YOU Your local city council member, our state governor, and a U.S. Supreme Court justice all serve you. But they each serve at different levels of government: local, state, and federal. What does each level of government represent?

Preview the Lesson

Vocabulary

jurisdiction *(n.)* the area over which an authority has control

branch *(n.)* a part of something

legislative branch *(n.)* the part of government responsible for making laws

executive branch *(n.)* the part of government responsible for carrying out laws

judicial branch *(n.)* the part of government responsible for deciding if laws have been broken

Vocabulary Activity The vocabulary words *legislative branch, executive branch,* and *judicial branch* are all related. How are they similar?

Reading: Compare and Contrast

Comparing and contrasting ideas will help you understand what you are reading. As you read page 144, underline the contrasts, or differences, among the three levels of government.

Levels of Government

In the United States there are three levels of government. Each level has a responsibility to serve the people. Each level of government also has a special jurisdiction. A **jurisdiction** is an area over which an authority has control.

The federal government has jurisdiction over certain areas. It is responsible for defending the United States. It runs the military and meets with governments of other nations. The federal government also takes care of national parks and monuments. It prints and watches over the nation's money supply too.

State governments have jurisdiction over other areas. They are responsible for guiding public education. They also take care of public health and safety.

Local governments provide services to cities, towns, and communities. These services include running police and fire departments, taking care of city parks, and keeping city records.

Each level of government has limits on what it can do. The Tenth Amendment to the U.S. Constitution says that any powers not given to the federal government in the Constitution are left to the states or the people. However, a state government cannot make a treaty, or agreement, with another country or pass laws that affect another state. A town's government cannot pass laws that go against state or federal laws.

1. List ways in which the duties of state and local governments are different. *Compare and Contrast*

State	Local

The U.S. Bureau of Printing and Engraving is responsible for printing our country's money.

The three branches of the federal government are all located in Washington, D.C.

Different Responsibilities

The federal government is made up of three separate branches. A **branch** is a part of something. All state governments also have three branches. These are the legislative, executive, and judicial branches. Each branch has different responsibilities.

At both the state and federal levels, the **legislative branch** is responsible for making laws. At the federal level, the Senate and the House of Representatives make up the legislative branch. Together they form Congress.

The **executive branch** of government is responsible for carrying out laws. In the federal government, the executive branch is led by the President of the United States. At both the federal and the state levels, the executive office is where bills are signed and become laws.

The **judicial branch** of government is responsible for interpreting laws and deciding if laws have been broken. It includes our system of courts and judges. At the federal level, the Supreme Court has power over all other courts in the country on matters that involve the Constitution. It is made up of nine justices, or judges.

2. List the important function of each branch of government below. *Main Ideas and Details*

Legislative

Executive

Judicial

Summary

Federal, state, and local governments have different responsibilities. How are the three levels of government alike?

Citizenship

Government Duties and Services

Learn More Below is a table that lists some of the responsibilities of local, state, and federal governments. As you read the table, think about why each level of government might be in charge of a particular duty or service.

Use the table to answer the questions below.

1. **Complete the table by writing in the level of government above each column.** *Identify*

2. **Why do you think fire protection is best handled at the local level rather than the federal level?** *Explain*

____

____

Three Levels of Government

	______	______	______
Protection	Utilizes local police and fire departments	Utilizes state police department	Utilizes Army, Navy, Marines, and Coast Guard
Education	Elects school leaders	Provides funding and guidelines for learning standards and educational materials	Provides funding and hiring guidelines
Parks	Funds and maintains local parks	Funds and maintains state parks	Funds and maintains national parks
Highways	Funds and maintains local roads	Funds and maintains state highways	Funds and maintains interstate highways
Treasury			Prints money

Name:

H-SS 4.5.4 Explain the structures and functions of state governments, including the roles and responsibilities of their elected officials.

Lesson 4

What does our state government do for us?

CONNECT TO YOU Who do you think makes the laws of our state? Who puts them into action? Who decides whether or not they are constitutional? California's government has three branches that oversee these responsibilities. How do these branches work together?

Preview the Lesson

Vocabulary

function *(n.)* a purpose

vote *(v.)* to express your choice for something or someone which results in a decision

election *(n.)* an event in which people vote to choose a person for an official position

Vocabulary Activity Complete the sentence with one of the vocabulary words above. *A CD player's* ____________ *is to play CDs.*

Reading: Fact and Opinion

Reading Skill

You have learned that a *fact* is something that is generally believed to be true. As you read page 148, underline facts about the legislative branch of the government.

Branches of State Government

You have learned about the legislative, executive, and judicial branches of the federal government. These branches are also part of California's state government. Each branch performs an important **function,** or purpose.

The legislative branch is made up of the state senate and state assembly. These groups write and vote on bills that affect people's lives. To **vote** is to express your choice for something or someone which results in a decision. The legislative branch also votes on constitutional amendments and resolutions, or official statements of opinions or ideas.

The executive branch carries out the laws created by the legislative branch. The governor leads this branch. He or she approves bills and makes sure laws are obeyed. One famous California governor was Ronald Reagan, who took office in 1967. Reagan later became the President of the United States in 1981.

In the judicial branch, judges make sure that laws are in line with the California Constitution. The judicial branch includes all the state courts in California.

1. Fact and Opinion **Based on this section, write an opinion statement about the government of California.**

Ronald Reagan became California's governor in 1967.

Arnold Schwarzenegger became governor of California in 2003.

The judicial branch of California's government provides a check on the other two branches.

Checks and Balances

Like the federal branches, the three branches of California's government have different duties. There is a system of checks and balances so that each branch has the power to set *checks,* or limits, on the powers of the other two. This helps keep a *balance* of power between branches.

Under this system, all three branches work together to serve the people. For example, the legislative branch can write and pass a bill, but the governor can either reject it or sign it into law. Judges decide if the law is constitutional, fitting with the ideas of our state's constitution.

The citizens of California can help maintain checks and balances by voting in elections. An **election** is an event in which people vote to choose a person for an official position. Citizens elect leaders who they think will make good decisions for the state. If our state's citizens do not think the leaders are making good decisions, they have the right to recall, or remove them from office. They can also elect new leaders.

2. Use the process of passing a bill to explain how the branches of government check one another. *Main Idea and Details*

Summary

California's government is organized into three branches with different responsibilities. How do citizens who vote help maintain the government's checks and balances?

Citizenship

California State Government

Learn More Each branch of California's state government has different duties, responsibilities, and requirements. As a result, no branch of the government holds too much power. Look at the chart, which lists the duties, requirements, and terms for the leaders of each branch of government.

LEGISLATIVE	EXECUTIVE	JUDICIAL
Duty: Writes laws	Duty: Approves and carries out laws	Duty: Interprets laws
State Assembly 80 members • Elected by the people of California • U.S. citizen • Has lived in California for past 3 years[1] • Serves for 2 years • Can be elected 3 times **State Senate** 40 members • Elected by the people of California • U.S. citizen • Has lived in California for past 3 years[1] • Serves for 4 years • Can be elected twice	**Governor** • Elected by the people of California • U.S. citizen • Has lived in California for past 5 years • Serves for 4 years • Can be elected twice	**State Supreme Court** 7 judges • Appointed by the governor, but reelected by the people of California • Has been a lawyer practicing in California for past 10 years or judge on a California court for past 10 years • Serves for 12 years

[1] and at least 1 year in his or her district

Use the chart above to answer the questions below:

1. **Circle the amount of time a person may serve on the state supreme court.** *Identify*
2. **Underline the requirement for the office of governor that is different from the requirements for members of the state senate.** *Apply*

Name:

H-SS 4.5.5 Describe the components of California's governance structure (e.g., cities and towns, Indian rancherias and reservations, counties, school districts).

Lesson 5

How are California's communities governed?

CONNECT TO YOU Every day you can see your local government in action around you. Local governments are smaller than state and federal governments. Often they can respond more easily to the people they serve. Can you think of examples of your local government working for you?

Preview the Lesson

Vocabulary

mayor *(n.)* a leader of a city or town

city council *(n.)* a group of people who make laws for the city

reservation *(n.)* an area of land owned by American Indian groups

rancheria *(n.)* a small reservation

district *(n.)* a part of a county, city, or state that is marked off for a special purpose

superintendent *(n.)* someone who is responsible for running all the schools in an area

school board *(n.)* a group of people who help manage the schools in an area

Vocabulary Activity The word *reservation* has more than one meaning. What is another definition for the word?

Reading: Fact and Opinion

Reading Skill

Remember that a *fact* is something that is generally believed to be true. As you read the second paragraph on page 152, underline facts about city governments.

Sukhee Kang, mayor of Irvine, poses with a student.

Local Government

Like our federal and state governments, local governments serve and protect the people. There are different types of local government in California. Cities and towns are often run by a mayor. The **mayor** is the leader of a city or town. Most communities also have a **city council,** which is a group of people who make laws for the city. The mayor and the city council work together to help the community. Counties are usually larger areas of the state that also have their own governments. Some cities, such as Los Angeles, are so large that they are their own counties.

Local governments are smaller than state or federal governments. This allows them to work closely with the people they serve. A local government offers important services to the community. For example, city governments provide police and fire protection. They also repair and clean streets. County governments often care for highways and roads. Citizens can help out at all levels by voting in elections and volunteering.

1. Fact and Opinion **List two facts to support the following statement: Cities and towns are served by their local government.**

Tribal Government

Some California Indian groups use a form of local government called a tribal council. Tribal councils may govern tribal land such as a **reservation,** which is an area of land owned by an American Indian group. A tribal council works with other governments to serve its people. The tribal chief is the head of the council and leads the community. Some small reservations, called **rancherias,** are also run by tribal councils.

School Districts

Another type of local government is a school district. A **district** is a part of a county, city, or state marked off for a special purpose. Most public schools are part of a school district. A **superintendent** is often responsible for running the public schools within a district. An elected school board may work with the superintendent. A **school board** is a group of people who help manage the schools in an area. A school's principal makes sure that his or her school follows the superintendent's and board's decisions.

A principal works with the superintendent, school board, and teachers and students to keep the school running smoothly.

2. How is the government of a reservation similar to other local governments?
Compare and Contrast

3. List the people who are responsible for running the schools in a school district.
Main Idea and Details

Summary

California has different kinds of local governments. Describe each of the local governments in our state.

Citizenship

Agua Caliente Tribal Council

Learn More The Agua Caliente Band of Cahuilla live in the Colorado Desert of Southern California. They call the area where they live Se-Khi, or "boiling water," because of the hot springs nearby. The Spanish named the area Agua Caliente, or "hot water." Today, the cities of Palm Springs, Cathedral City, and Rancho Mirage, as well as Riverside County, are located in the Agua Caliente reservation.

In 1876 the United States recognized nine reservations for the Cahuilla, including the Agua Caliente reservation. In 1952 the Agua Caliente voted to approve their own constitution. The Tribal Council runs the government on the reservation. The Tribal Council makes laws and protects the interests of its people. It manages the area's land and businesses. It also takes care of the wildlife and natural resources around the reservation. The Tribal Council helps preserve the arts and culture of its people. One way it has done this is by working with the community to build a museum that presents the history and traditions of the Cahuilla.

Answer the questions below.

1. **Circle the responsibilities of the Agua Caliente Cahuilla Tribal Council.** *Identify*
2. **Name one way in which the Tribal Council is like the other local governments you have read about.** *Analyze*

____

____

Agua Caliente Cultural Museum in Palm Springs, CA

Table of Contents

Atlas
Map of Our Fifty States: Political

CANADA
Lake Superior
Lake Michigan
Lake Huron
Lake Ontario
Lake Erie
NORTH DAKOTA (ND)
Grand Forks
Bismarck
Fargo
SOUTH DAKOTA (SD)
Pierre
Sioux Falls
Missouri
River
NEBRASKA (NE)
Omaha
Lincoln
KANSAS (KS)
Kansas City
Topeka
Wichita
OKLAHOMA (OK)
Tulsa
Oklahoma City
TEXAS (TX)
Fort Worth
Dallas
Austin
San Antonio
Houston
Laredo
Corpus Christi
MINNESOTA (MN)
Duluth
Minneapolis
St. Paul
IOWA (IA)
Cedar Rapids
Davenport
Des Moines
MISSOURI (MO)
Kansas City
Jefferson City
St. Louis
ARKANSAS (AR)
Fort Smith
Little Rock
LOUISIANA (LA)
Shreveport
Baton Rouge
New Orleans
WISCONSIN (WI)
Green Bay
Madison
Milwaukee
ILLINOIS (IL)
Rockford
Chicago
Peoria
Springfield
Mississippi
River
MICHIGAN (MI)
Grand Rapids
Lansing
Detroit
INDIANA (IN)
Gary
Fort Wayne
Indianapolis
Evansville
OHIO (OH)
Toledo
Cleveland
Columbus
Cincinnati
Ohio
River
KENTUCKY (KY)
Louisville
Frankfort
TENNESSEE (TN)
Nashville
Knoxville
Memphis
MISSISSIPPI (MS)
Jackson
Biloxi
ALABAMA (AL)
Birmingham
Montgomery
Mobile
GEORGIA (GA)
Atlanta
Columbus
Savannah
FLORIDA (FL)
Tallahassee
Jacksonville
Tampa
Miami
SOUTH CAROLINA (SC)
Columbia
Charleston
NORTH CAROLINA (NC)
Raleigh
Charlotte
VIRGINIA (VA)
Richmond
Norfolk
WEST VIRGINIA (WV)
Charleston
Wheeling
PENNSYLVANIA (PA)
Pittsburgh
Harrisburg
Philadelphia
NEW YORK (NY)
Buffalo
Albany
New York
NEW HAMPSHIRE (NH)
VERMONT (VT)
Burlington
Montpelier
Concord
MAINE (ME)
Augusta
Portland
MASSACHUSETTS (MA)
Boston
Providence
RHODE ISLAND (RI)
Hartford
CONNECTICUT (CT)
Newark
Trenton
NEW JERSEY (NJ)
Baltimore
Dover
DELAWARE (DE)
Annapolis
MARYLAND (MD)
Washington, D.C.
ATLANTIC OCEAN
Gulf of Mexico
BAHAMAS
N
50°N
40°N
30°N
70°W
80°W
90°W

Atlas
Map of California: Physical

Glossary

This glossary will help you understand the meanings of and pronounce the vocabulary words in this book. The page number tells you where the word first appears.

A

absolute location (ab′sə lüt lō kā′shən), *n.* the exact or nearly exact location of a place on Earth using degrees north or south and east or west (p. 3)

actor (ak′tər), *n.* a person who performs in plays, movies, or television shows (p. 129)

aerospace (âr′ō spās), *n.* the science of flight (p. 117)

agriculture (ag′rə kul′chər), *n.* the growing of crops and raising of animals (p. 23)

amendment (ə mend′mənt), *n.* a change or addition (p. 135)

aqueduct (ak′wə dukt), *n.* a pipe or other system that brings water from a distance (p. 117)

architecture (är′kə tek′chər), *n.* the style and design of a building (p. 23)

B

bay (bā), *n.* a part of a sea or lake that cuts into a coastline (p. 121)

belief (bi lēf′), *n.* something held as true or real (p. 31)

boomtown (büm′toun′), *n.* a town that grows rapidly as a result of new business (p. 75)

border (bôr′dər), *n.* an official line that separates one place from another (p. 19)

boundary (boun′dər ē), *n.* a line or natural feature that separates one area, state, or country from another (p. 57)

branch (branch), *n.* a part of something (p. 143)

C

capital (kap′ə təl), *n.* a city where a country's or state's central government is located (p. 11)

Catholicism (kə thol′ə siz′əm), *n.* the religion of the Catholic Church (p. 41)

citizenship (sit′ə zən ship), *n.* the duties, rights, and responsibilities of individuals living in a state or country (p. 139)

city council (sit′ē koun′səl), *n.* a group of people who make laws for the city (p. 151)

climate (klī′mit), *n.* the weather patterns in one place over a long period of time (p. 7)

coast (kōst), *n.* the land along an ocean (p. 11)

college (kol′ij), *n.* a school where people study after high school (p. 125)

colony (kol′ə nē), *n.* a settlement of people who come from one country to live in another land (p. 41)

communication (kə myü′nə kā′shən), *n.* the way that people send and receive information (p. 91)

compass rose (kum′pəs rōz), *n.* a symbol that shows the main directions on a map (p. 3)

compromise (kom′prə mīz), *n.* a solution to a disagreement in which each side gives up a part of what it wants (p. 81)

Pronunciation Key

a	in hat	ō	in open	sh	in she
ā	in age	ȯ	in all	th	in thin
â	in care	ô	in order	ᴛʜ	in then
ä	in far	oi	in oil	zh	in measure
e	in let	ou	in out	ə	= a in about
ē	in equal	u	in cup	ə	= e in taken
ėr	in term	ů	in put	ə	= i in pencil
i	in it	ü	in rule	ə	= o in lemon
ī	in ice	ch	in child	ə	= u in circus
o	in hot	ng	in long		

Glossary

constitution (kon′stə tü′shən), *n.* a written plan for governing a country or state (p. 85)

convention (kən ven′shən), *n.* a large meeting arranged for a special purpose (p. 135)

cultivate (kul′tə vāt), *v.* to prepare and use land to grow crops (p. 53)

culture (kul′chər), *n.* the customs, arts, entertainment, and recreation of a group (p. 129)

current (kėr′ənt), *n.* the pattern of the flow of water (p. 37)

custom (kus′təm), *n.* a way a group of people does something (p. 31)

D

dam (dam), *n.* a wall built to hold back water (p. 53)

degree (di grē′), *n.* a rank or title given to someone who has completed a program of study at a school (p. 125)

delegate (del′ə git), *n.* a person who is chosen to speak for others (p. 85)

delta (del′tə), *n.* an area of land where a river separates into smaller rivers flowing into a body of water (p. 121)

depression (di presh′ən), *n.* a period when there is little business activity and many people do not have jobs (p. 111)

desert (dez′ərt), *n.* an area that receives less than ten inches of rain in one year (p. 11)

discrimination (dis krim′ə nā′shən), *n.* treating someone differently from someone else in an unfair way (p. 97)

district (dis′trikt), *n.* a part of a county, city, or state that is marked off for a special purpose (p. 151)

diversity (də vėr′sə tē), *n.* many different types of people or things (p. 97)

drought (drout), *n.* a long period of time without rain (p. 111)

E

economy (i kon′ə mē), *n.* the system of producing and consuming goods in a country, state, or local area (p. 49)

election (i lek′shən), *n.* an event in which people vote to choose a person for an official position (p. 147)

engineer (en′jə nir′), *n.* a person who designs structures such as roads, bridges, and machines (p. 91)

entrepreneur (än′trə prə nėr′ *or* än′trə prə nůr′), *n.* a person who starts a new business with the hope of making money (p. 75)

equator (i kwā′tər), *n.* the line of latitude that circles the middle of Earth (p. 3)

exclusion (ek sklü′zhən), *n.* the act of keeping something or someone out (p. 103)

executive branch (eg zek′yə tiv branch), *n.* the part of government responsible for carrying out laws (p. 143)

expand (ek spand′), *v.* to grow larger (p. 71)

expedition (ek′spə dish′ən), *n.* a journey made for a special purpose (p. 41)

explore (ek splôr′), *v.* to travel to places in order to learn more about them (p. 37)

export (ek′spôrt), *v.* to send something to another country or area to be sold (p. 97)

F

fort (fôrt), *n.* a building used by soldiers to defend an important place (p. 45)

fugitive (fyü′jə tiv), *n.* a person who tries to escape from an authority (p. 81)

function (fungk′shən), *n.* a purpose (p. 147)

G

government (guv′ərn mənt), *n.* a country's laws and leaders (p. 57)

Glossary

H

hemisphere (hem′ə sfir), *n.* one half of Earth (p. 7)

hunter-gatherer (hun′tər gaᴛʜ′ər ər), *n.* a person who gets food by hunting animals and gathering plants (p. 53)

I

immigrate (im′ə grāt), *v.* to come into another country to live (p. 71)

import (im′pôrt), *v.* to bring something in from another country or area to sell (p. 97)

inflation (in flā′shən), *n.* when prices rise (p. 111)

investor (in ves′tər), *n.* a person who gives money to a company with the hope of making money later (p. 91)

irrigation (ir′ə gā′shən), *n.* the use of pipes or ditches to bring water to where it is needed (p. 53)

J

judicial branch (jü dish′əl branch), *n.* the part of government responsible for deciding if laws have been broken (p. 143)

jurisdiction (jür′is dik′shən), *n.* the area over which an authority has control (p. 143)

L

landform (land′fôrm′), *n.* a natural feature of Earth's surface (p. 11)

land grant (land grant), *n.* land given by a government (p. 49)

legend (lej′ənd), *n.* an old, well-known story (p. 31)

legislative branch (lej′ə slā′tiv branch), *n.* the part of government responsible for making laws (p. 143)

line of latitude (līn uv lat′ə tüd), *n.* an imaginary line that runs east-west around Earth (p. 3)

line of longitude (līn uv lon′jə tüd), *n.* an imaginary line that runs from the North Pole to the South Pole (p. 3)

M

mayor (mā′ər), *n.* a leader of a city or town (p. 151)

merchant (mėr′chənt), *n.* a person who buys and sells goods (p. 97)

migrant worker (mī′grant wėr′kər), *n.* person who regularly moves from place to place to do a job (p. 107)

migrate (mī′grāt), *v.* to move from one place to another (p. 71)

mission (mish′ən), *n.* a settlement set up by a religious group to teach their religion and other ways of life to native people (p. 41)

missionary (mish′ə ner′ē), *n.* a person who teaches his or her religion to people who have different beliefs (p. 41)

mountain pass (moun′tən pas), *n.* a narrow gap in a mountain range (p. 19)

N

natural resource (nach′ər əl rē′sôrs), *n.* a useful material that comes from the earth (p. 19)

Pronunciation Key

a	in hat	ō	in open	sh	in she
ā	in age	ȯ	in all	th	in thin
â	in care	ô	in order	ᴛʜ	in then
ä	in far	oi	in oil	zh	in measure
e	in let	ou	in out	ə	= a in about
ē	in equal	u	in cup	ə	= e in taken
ėr	in term	ů	in put	ə	= i in pencil
i	in it	ü	in rule	ə	= o in lemon
ī	in ice	ch	in child	ə	= u in circus
o	in hot	ng	in long		

Glossary

nonrenewable resource (non′ri nü′ə bəl rē′sôrs), *n.* a resource that comes from the earth and cannot be replaced (p. 121)

O

occupy (ok′yə pī), *v.* to take control of a place (p. 49)

P

petition (pə tish′ən), *v.* to officially ask someone to do something (p. 81)

pioneer (pī′ə nir′), *n.* a person who is one of the first settlers of a part of a country (p. 67)

population density (pop′yə lā′shən den′sə tē), *n.* the average number of people living in a specific unit of area (p. 23)

presidio (pri sid′ē ō), *n.* a Spanish word for fort (p. 49)

prime meridian (prīm mə rid′ē ən), *n.* Earth's main line of longitude (p. 3)

principle (prin′sə pəl), *n.* an important belief (p. 135)

private (prī′vit), *adj.* not owned by the government (p. 125)

product (prod′əkt), *n.* something that is made, grown, or taken from nature and sold (p. 97)

public (pub′lik), *adj.* available for anyone to use (p. 125)

pueblo (pweb′lō), *n.* a Spanish word for village (p. 49)

R

rancheria (ran′chə rē′ə), *n.* a small reservation (p. 151)

rancho (ran′chō), *n.* a large area of land where crops are grown and horses, cattle, sheep, and pigs are raised (p. 49)

ratify (rat′ə fī), *v.* to officially approve (p. 85)

ration (rash′ən or rā′shən), *v.* to allow people only a limited amount of something because there is not enough of it (p. 111)

region (rē′jən), *n.* a large area in which places share similar features (p. 11)

religion (ri lij′ən), *n.* a system of faith and worship (p. 31)

renewable resource (ri nü′ə bəl rē′sôrs), *n.* a resource which can be replaced (p. 121)

representative (rep′ri zen′tə tiv), *n.* someone who is chosen to act for someone else (p. 85)

republic (ri pub′lik), *n.* a type of government in which citizens elect leaders to represent them (p. 85)

reservation (rez′ər vā′shən), *n.* an area of land owned by American Indian groups (p. 151)

reservoir (rez′ər vwär), *n.* a place where water is collected and stored for use (p. 121)

responsibility (ri spon′sə bil′ə tē), *n.* a duty or something that must be done (p. 135)

rural area (rùr′əl âr′ē ə), *n.* an area of small towns or farms (p. 23)

S

school board (skül bôrd), *n.* a group of people who help manage the schools in an area (p. 151)

settle (set′l), *v.* to move to and set up a new place to live (p. 19)

slavery (slā′vər ē), *n.* the practice of owning people and forcing them to work without pay (p. 81)

squatter (skwät′ər), *n.* a person who settles on land he or she does not own (p. 103)

stock market (stok mär′kit), *n.* the business of buying and selling shares of companies (p. 111)

strike (strīk), *n.* when workers refuse to do their job until their demands are met (p. 103)

suburban area (sə bėr′bən âr′ē ə), *n.* an area just outside a city (p. 23)

superintendent (sü′pər in ten′dənt), *n.* someone who is responsible for running all the schools in an area (p. 151)

Glossary

T

tax (taks), *n.* money the government collects to pay for its services (p. 61)

technology (tek nol′ə jē), *n.* the use of scientific knowledge to solve problems (p. 91)

telegraph (tel′ə graf), *n.* a machine that sends signals along wires using electricity (p. 91)

territory (ter′ə tôr′ē), *n.* a geographic area that relies on an outside government but usually has some independence (p. 57)

trade (trād), *v.* to exchange goods and services (p. 31)

trade school (trād skül), *n.* a place where people learn how to do a job (p. 125)

tradition (trə dish′ən), *n.* a special way that a group does something, which is part of their way of life (p. 31)

transportation (tran′spər tā′shən), *n.* the moving of goods, people, or animals from one place to another (p. 23)

Tropic of Cancer (trop′ik əv kan′sər), *n.* the northernmost point where the sun shines directly overhead (p. 7)

Tropic of Capricorn (trop′ik əv kap′rə kôrn), *n.* the southernmost point where the sun shines directly overhead (p. 7)

U

university (yü′nə vėr′sə tē), *n.* the highest level of school from which you can earn a degree (p. 125)

urban area (ėr′bən âr′ē ə), *n.* a city area (p. 23)

V

vote (vōt), *v.* to express your choice for something or someone which results in a decision (p. 147)

Pronunciation Key

a	in hat	ō	in open	sh	in she
ā	in age	ȯ	in all	th	in thin
â	in care	ô	in order	ᴛʜ	in then
ä	in far	oi	in oil	zh	in measure
e	in let	ou	in out	ə	= a in about
ē	in equal	u	in cup	ə	= e in taken
ėr	in term	ů	in put	ə	= i in pencil
i	in it	ü	in rule	ə	= o in lemon
ī	in ice	ch	in child	ə	= u in circus
o	in hot	ng	in long		

Index

This Index lists the pages on which topics appear in this book. Page numbers after an *m* refer to a map. The terms *See* and *See also* will direct you to additional entries.

Index

Index

Index

Credits

Text

Excerpt from 'Diary of Pedro Font', November 1, 1775 from *Anza's California Expeditions 5 vols.* Copyright © 1930 The Regents of the University of California. Reprinted by permission. p. 56

Excerpt from "49er: Memories Recalled Years Later for Her Daughter" by Correnah Wilson Wright. Copyright © 1937, Eucalyptus Press of Mills College. Reprinted by permission. p. 80

Illustrations

1, 4, 5, 9, 12, 20, 24, 25, 28, 32, 38, 42, 46, 58, 68, 72, 76, 78, 82, 86, 92, 93, 94, 104, 112, 114, 119, 122, 136, 140, 156, 158 Mapquest, Inc.; **13** Cheryl Mendenhall; **15** Andrea Z. Tachiera; **50, 124** Robert Lawson.

Photographs

Every effort has been made to secure permission and provide appropriate credit for photographic material. The publisher deeply regrets any omission and pledges to correct errors called to its attention in subsequent editions.

Unless otherwise acknowledged, all photographs are the property of Pearson Education, Inc.

Photo locators denoted as follows: Top (T), Center (C), Bottom (B), Left (L), Right (R), Background (Bkgd)

Front Matter: **i** (T) Charles O'Rear/Corbis, (Bkgd) Spencer Grant/PhotoEdit; **ii** (C) ©J.M. Dunn/Robertstock, (T) ©The Irvine Museum; **iii** ©Bruce Burkhardt/Corbis, (T) From the collection of the SFMTA Archives.; **iv** (T) ©Neil Lukas/DK Images, (T) SuperStock; **v** (B) ©Japanese American Archival Collection. Department of Special Collections and University Archives, Library/California State University, Sacramento, (C) ©Lee Foster/Lonely Planet Images; **vi** (Bkgd) Richard Cummins/ Corbis;

Unit 1: **7** (C) ©Nora Good/Masterfile Corporation; **10** Tim Davis/Corbis; **11** Harvey Lloyd/Getty Images; **12** (B) Radius Images / Alamy; **13** (T) Ellen Isaacs /Alamy; **14** (BR) ©Alan Schein, (C) ©Henryk T. Kaiser/Getty Images, (CL) ©Pete Saloutos/Corbis, Harold Sund/Getty Images; **15** (CR) ©John Elk III/Photoshot, (CL) ©Joseph Sohm; ChromoSohm Inc/Corbis, (C) Dennis Hallinan/Alamy Images, (B) Elizabeth Holmes/OmniPhoto/Universal Images Group, (CL) Nik Wheeler, (CL) Photoshot, (TR, BR) Shutterstock; **16** (C) SuperStock/Alamy Images; **17** Charles O'Rear/Corbis;

Unit 2: **21** (T) ©Ed Young/Corbis; **22** (CL) Brown Brothers, (R) Ronnie Kaufman/Corbis; **23** Ted Streshinsky/Corbis; **24** (R) Corbis Premium RF/Alamy; **25** (B) ©Robert Campbell/SuperStock; **26** (Inset) C. Moore/Corbis, (B) Spencer Grant/ PhotoEdit; **27** Bruce Burkhardt/Corbis; **31** (Bkgd) ©Lawrence Migdale; **33** (BL) bpk, Berlin/Dietrich Graf/Art Resource, NY, Chuck Place/Alamy Images; **34** ©The Granger Collection, NY; **35** (T) ©Lawrence Migdale; **36** (BR) Getty Images; **37** ©Courtesy of the Bancroft Library, University of California, Berkeley; **39** The Granger Collection, NY; **40** (CR) The Granger Collection, NY; **41** (C) Corbis; **42** (B) ©Lee Foster/Lonely Planet Images, (T) ©Seaver Center for Western History Research; **43** North Wind Picture Archives/Alamy Images; **44** (BR) ©Lake County Museum/Corbis; **46** ©Michael Maslan Historic Photographs/ Corbis; **47** (TR) ©The Irvine Museum; **48** Richard Cummins/ Robert Harding Picture Library Ltd/ Alamy Images; **49** Thomas Barrat/Shutterstock; **51** (CR) ©Phil Schermeister/Corbis; **53** Sienna Van Nostrand/Alamy; **54** (CR) ©The Granger Collection, NY, (BL) Aurora Photos/Alamy Images; **55** (CR) ©Lowell Georgia/Corbis; **56** (C) BANC MSS M-M 1725, Page 2/©Courtesy of the Bancroft Library, University of California, Berkeley; **57** Art Resource, NY; **58** (BR) The Granger Collection, NY; **59** (CR) The Granger Collection, NY; **60** (BR) AP/Wide World Photos; **61** ©George H. H. Huey/Corbis; **62** (BR) The Granger Collection, NY; **63** (T) ©Bonnie Kamin/ PhotoEdit; **64** (C) ©Earth Science & Map Library/ University of California, Berkeley;

Unit 3: **67** (C) ©Dave G. Houser/Corbis; **68** Andrew McKinney/©DK Images; **69** (TL) The Granger Collection, NY; **71** (C) Getty Images; **72** (BL) ©Villa Farnese, Caprarola, Lazio, Italy, Giraudon/Bridgeman Art Library; **73** (C) ©Archives Charmet/Bridgeman Art Library, (TR) The Granger Collection, NY; **74** (BL) James Steinberg /Photo Researchers, Inc.; **75** (C) ©John Cancalosi/ Stock, Boston Inc/Jupiter Images; **76** ABN IMAGES/Alamy Images; **77** (T) The Granger Collection, NY; **78** (CR) Corbis, (BL) Getty Images; **79** (CR) Levi Strauss & Co., (C) Nancy Richmond/ Image Works; **80** (TR) ©Carl Mautz; **81** North Wind Picture Archives; **82** (BC) Corbis; **83** (TR) ©Permission granted by Jack Kim/Berkeley Architectural Heritage Association; **84** (C) The Granger Collection, NY; **85** (C) ©J.M. Dunn/ Robertstock; **87** (BR) Call number 1899.001 03—fALB/©Courtesy of the Bancroft Library, University of California, Berkeley;

Unit 4: **91** (C) SuperStock; **92** (BR) ©Hulton Archive/Getty Images; **93** (BR) ©National Museum of American History/Neg.#74-2491/ National Museum of American History/ Smithsonian Institution, (TR) The Granger Collection, NY; **95** (TL) ©Courtesy of the California History Room, California State Library, Sacramento CA, (TR) Bettmann/ Corbis; **96** (C) Bettmann/Corbis; **97** (CR) ©Bettmann/Corbis, (C) Bettmann/Corbis; **98** (B) Corbis; **99** (B) From the collection of the SFMTA Archives.; **100** (B) ©Japanese American Archival Collection. Department of Special Collections and University Archives, Library/California State University, Sacramento; **101** (T) Corbis, (CR) The Granger Collection, NY; **103** (C) ©Detail of Image 231-18-013, Courtesy of California State Parks, 2004/California State Parks; **104** (BR) ©Courtesy of the California History Room, California State Library, Sacramento CA; **105** (T) Courtesy of California State Parks, 2004. Image 090-711; **106** (TR) National Archives; **107** (C) The Granger Collection, NY; **108** (BR) Corbis; **109** (T) ©Paul Conklin/ PhotoEdit; **110** (BR) ©1976 George Ballis/ Take Stock, (CR) CSU Archives/Everett Collection/Alamy Images; **111** (C) Corbis; **112** (BR) Brown Brothers, (Bkgd) Corbis, (C) Minnesota Historical Society/Corbis; **113** (BR) Corbis; **114** (CR) Courtesy of FDR Library, Hyde Park, NY; **115** Collection Center for Creative Photography, University of Arizona ©The Ansel Adams Publishing Rights Trust/ Library of Congress, (TL) Gift of Jack and Peggy Iwata, Japanese American National Museum (93.102.123); **116** (CR) ©Island Mountain Trading Company, (R) ©Susan Ahn Cuddy Collection/Island Mountain Trading Company; **117** (C) Corbis; **118** (BR) Brown Brothers; **120** (CR) ©JSC Digital Image Collection/NASA, (TR, CR) Getty Images; **121** (C) ©Bob Rowan/Corbis; **122** (B) ©Simon Wilkinson/Getty Images; **125** ©Myrleen Pearson/Alamy Images; **126** (T) Online Archive of California/1996.003 v/28:71b- -fALB/©Courtesy of the Bancroft Library, University of California, Berkeley; **127** (CR) John Elk III; **129** (C) ©Robert Landau/Corbis; **130** (BC) ©Gary Conner/Getty Images; **131** (CR) Corbis, (C) SuperStock; **132** (BL) ©Allstar Picture Library/Alamy Images, (CR) NewsCom;

Unit 5: **135** (C) ©Bettmann/Corbis; **136** ©Robert Mullan/Alamy; **137** (TR) The Granger Collection, NY, WorldFoto/ Alamy Images; **138** (TR) Aaron Haupt/ Photo Researchers, Inc.; **139** (C) ©Bill Aron/ PhotoEdit; **140** (TR) ©California State Archives; **141** (TC) ©Robyn Beck/AFP/Getty Images; **142** (BR) ©Neil Lukas/DK Images; **143** (C) ©Warner J. Bertsch/Photoshot; **144** (BR) AP/Wide World Photos; **146** (BC) ©Penni Gladstone/San Francisco Chronicle/ Corbis, (BR, BL) AP/Wide World Photos; **147** (C) AP/Wide World Photos; **148** (CR) ©Courtesy Ronald Reagan Library, (BC) AP/Wide World Photos; **149** (T) ©Mark Richards/PhotoEdit; **150** (B) Judicial Council of California/California Courts, The Judicial Branch of California; **151** (CR) AP/Wide World Photos; **152** Kevin Sullivan/The Orange County Register/ZUMAPRESS/NewsCom; **153** (BR) ©Michael Newman/PhotoEdit; **154** ©M. Sobreira/Alamy Images; **155** (B) ©Spencer Grant/Stock, Boston Inc./Jupiter Images.